Your
Horoscope
2020

. . . .

Aquarius

Your Horoscope 2020

Aquarius

21st January - 19th February

igloobooks

igloobooks

Published in 2019
by Igloo Books Ltd
Cottage Farm
Sywell
NN6 0BJ
www.igloobooks.com

0819 001.01
2 4 6 8 10 9 7 5 3 1
ISBN 978-1-78905-709-6

Written by Belinda Campbell and Jennifer Zelinger

Cover design by Dave Chapman
Edited by Bobby Newlyn-Jones

Printed and manufactured in China

CONTENTS

INTRODUCTION
··················

This horoscope has been specifically created to allow
you to get the most from astrological patterns and
the way they have a bearing on not only your zodiac
sign, but nuances within it. Using the diary section
of the book you can read about the influences and
possibilities of each and every day of the year. It will
be possible for you to see when you are likely to be
cheerful and happy or those times when your nature
is in retreat and you will be more circumspect. The
diary will help to give you a feel for the specific
'cycles' of astrology and the way they can subtly
change your day-to-day life.

THE CHARACTER OF
THE WATER BEARER
....

A rebel in the style of James Dean, with or without a
cause, Aquarius is the Water Bearer sign of the zodiac
that is here to give to their communities whilst also
making waves. With the rebellious songs of the sixties in
their ear, breaking tradition and challenging conventions
is what this free-thinking Air sign is all about. Whilst
the songs of the 1960s might lay claim to the age of
Aquarius, no one can quite agree on when this sign's
astrological age begins or ends. An astrological age
is thought to be close to 2000 years long and defined
by the associated sign, so why is the age of Aquarius
the one that everyone makes a song and dance about?
Belonging to the eleventh house in the zodiac calendar
that represents community and friendship, Aquarians
and their astrological age are sure to influence and
change up the whole world and everyone in it as this
sign is about realising common goals, hopes and dreams
for the future.

Co-ruled by rule-abiding Saturn and rebellious Uranus,
Aquarians can be unapologetic when it comes to
breaking tradition and will march to the beat of their
own drum alone if they must, whether that's to the
reggae beat of Bob Marley or the classical compositions
of Mozart. Born in the middle of winter, fixed Aquarians
may be set in their way of thinking, rightly or wrongly.
With a positive energy, Aquarians can be wonderful
at acting on what they believe. Aquarian activists Rosa

Parks with her Montgomery Bus Boycott and Yoko
Ono with her bed-ins for peace show how this sign
can act against injustices. Aquarians are known for
being progressive thinkers, with an eye fixed firmly
on the future, which is perhaps why technological
advancements are often closely linked with this
futuristic sign. With Aquarians' devotion to their social
responsibility and the speed at which technology is sky-
rocketing, the age of Aquarius may well be in full swing
as social media activism, or hashtivism, for example in
movements like #TimesUp which continue to gather
followers globally. With influential philanthropists
and activists like Aquarians Ellen DeGeneres and
Oprah Winfrey belonging to this star sign, the voice of
Aquarius is sure to be heard for decades to come.

THE WATER BEARER

Despite being an Air sign, it is the giving Water Bearer
that symbolises Aquarius. Ruled by Saturn who was
named after the Roman god of agriculture, Aquarius'
symbol of the Water Bearer shows the eternal current
of positive energy that flows from this sign and helps
the world to grow. The gifts of the Water Bearer can be
numerous, but this Air sign is likely to influence society
most substantially through their progressive thoughts
and ideas. Aquarians can be visionaries, and this Air
sign's alternative way of thinking combined with their
outgoing nature means that others are likely to listen to
what they have to say. Although not everyone may agree
with the rebel-minded Aquarius, this futuristic thinker
is usually ahead of their time, their symbol of the Water

Bearer suggests that what this sign will bring to the world will be given with the best of intentions for the goal of a brighter future.

SATURN AND URANUS

The second largest planet in the solar system, Saturn stands out as loud and proud as its co-ruled sign Aquarius. Belonging to the eleventh house of community, this Saturn ruled sign will likely take their social responsibility extremely seriously and may focus all their hard work into building a community that they believe to be just and fair. With the authority of Saturn co-guiding this sign, their fixed way of thinking can at times come across as a little preachy or superior, so this Air sign should try to always listen and remain open-minded. Co-ruled by radical Uranus, Aquarians may be all about change and liberation from the rules of Saturn. Uranus is known for its off-kilter axis which could go a long way to explaining the alternative and unconventional traits that some Aquarians can display. Saturn's size and Uranus' unique tilt make these two planets stand out in the solar system and could act as a reminder to all belonging to this extraordinary sign that Aquarians were born to be a little different.

ELEMENTS, MODES AND POLARITIES

Each sign is made up of a unique combination of three
defining groups: elements, modes and polarities. Each
of these defining parts can manifest themselves in good
and bad ways and none should be seen as a positive
or a negative – including the polarities! Just like a
jigsaw puzzle, piecing these groups together can help
illuminate why each sign has certain characteristics and
help us find a balance.

ELEMENTS

Fire: Dynamic and adventurous, signs with Fire in them
can be extroverted. Others are naturally drawn to them
because of the positive light they give off, as well as their
high levels of energy and confidence.

Earth: Signs with the Earth element are steady and
driven with their ambitions. They make for a solid
friend, parent or partner due to their grounded
influence and nurturing nature.

Air: The invisible element that influences each of the
other elements significantly, Air signs will provide
much-needed perspective to others with their fair
thinking, verbal skills and key ideas.

Water: Warm in the shallows and freezing as ice.
This mysterious element is essential to the growth of
everything around it, through its emotional depth
and empathy.

MODES

Cardinal: Pioneers of the calendar, cardinal signs jump-start each season and are the energetic go-getters.

Fixed: Marking the middle of the calendar, fixed signs firmly denote and value steadiness and reliability.

Mutable: As the seasons end, the mutable signs adapt and give themselves over gladly to the promise of change.

POLARITIES

Positive: Typically extroverted, positive signs take physical action and embrace outside stimulus in their life.

Negative: Usually introverted, negative signs value emotional development and experiencing life from the inside out.

AQUARIUS IN BRIEF

The table below shows the key attributes of Aquarians. Use it for quick reference and to understand more about this fascinating sign.

SYMBOL	RULING PLANET	MODE	ELEMENT	HOUSE
♒	♄ ♅	⊟	△	ⅪI
The Water Bearer	Saturn and Uranus	Fixed	Air	Eleventh

COLOUR	BODY PART	POLARITY	GENDER	POLAR SIGN
		⊕	♂	♌
Blue	Ankles and Circulation	Positive	Masculine	Leo

LOVE

Aquarians can be some of the friendliest and most alluring of all people and are unlikely to be short of admirers. They may have a laid-back approach to finding a partner, and if they are in a relationship can even seem aloof, but devotion is usually steadfast with this fixed sign. If an Aquarian is not overly emotional with their partner and is much happier to exchange thoughts and ideas than feelings, it is not necessarily because they are not emotionally invested in the relationship. A closed-off Aquarius could struggle with a Water sign partner and likewise, Water signs might not warm to the cool exterior of this Air sign. Warm and passionate Fire signs are sure to raise this Air sign's temperature and as these elements share a positive outgoing energy, plenty of common interests could be shared. As is the case with many Air signs, their love can feel like a trip to the heavens or a painful plummet to Earth. But even if this sign falls out of love, the friendships that they form can be so firm that they can withstand a break-up and be the rule breakers that do in fact stay friends with their exes.

Whilst being highly independent, Aquarians are all about teamwork so can truly thrive in a loving relationship so long as it stems from a firm friendship and mutual beliefs. This giving Water Bearer sign may struggle to give up their prized individualism in exchange for a partnership, and their fixed attitude can give them a stubborn edge that makes them resistant to accepting any dramatic changes to their lifestyle. A partner that understands their Aquarian's desire to remain autonomous and is fully accepting of their uniqueness is one that this sign should try and hold on to. A jealous or possessive lover is a big no-no for this free spirit. Aquarians who want to let love into their lives should understand that change is inevitable and what can feel like an upheaval to their independence is more of a loving revolution.

ARIES: COMPATIBILITY 3/5

Two signs known for their admirable quality of being a good friend to all, Aries and Aquarius should have a good solid foundation of friendship to base their romantic relationship on. This coupling of Air and Fire will always make for a fuelled love. Independence is key for keeping your Aquarius lover happy, so Aries should be careful with trying to control the relationship or forcing Aquarius to commit too soon. Whilst these two signs have many things in common, it will be discovering each other's differences that will be essential in keeping both partners interested in this relationship.

TAURUS: COMPATIBILITY 1/5

Taurus and Aquarius aren't an obvious match on paper – it's unlikely that these two will find each other on a matchmaking website! The core differences between these signs makes a romantic spark unlikely but should not be ruled out. Aquarius is partly ruled by the planet Uranus, symbolising rebellion and change, i.e. some Taureans' worst nightmare. For the easy life-seeking Taurus who likes what they know, the travel-lusting

Aquarius can be hard to keep up with. However, these two signs are both fixed and have the potential to make each other stronger if they remain open to change.

GEMINI: COMPATIBILITY 4/5

The individualist sign Aquarius and Twin sign Gemini can make for a compatible trio. Born in the eleventh house that signifies community and friendship, Aquarians thrive in groups and will be a fantastic partner to social butterfly Gemini. The mutable nature of Geminis will mean that they are happy to follow their Aquarian fixed lover's lead which will likely bring a steadiness to the relationship. Being both positive and Air signs, these two will have plenty in common. With a Gemini's love for change and an Aquarian's need for progress, these two could create a bright and revolutionary future together.

CANCER: COMPATIBILITY 1/5

The rebellious Aquarius and security seeking Cancer are not always an obvious match romantically. Whilst their core character differences may be the cause of arguments, if these two can find common interests that can cement a foundation for friendship then love could still bloom. If Cancer can help intellectual Aquarius give themselves emotionally to a partner, then both could mutually benefit from this unlikely but special meeting of the heart and mind. Find common ground to share and foreign lands to explore and Aquarius and Cancer could find a lasting love together.

LEO: COMPATIBILITY 5/5

Aquarius is the Air sign that sparks the embers of Leo's Fire element into full blaze. Opposites on the calendar, this combination of shared positive energy, fixed attitudes and complimentary elements make Leo and Aquarius two individuals that were astrologically made for each other. These unique characters can be guilty of feeling superior to others so may need to remind themselves to treat each other as their rightful equals. Foremost, this is a friendship sprung from fun and crafted by a shared creativity. The visionary mind of Leo combined with Aquarian ideals could have these two creating a utopic life together.

VIRGO: COMPATIBILITY 2/5

Idealist Aquarius and realist Virgo may not be an obvious match, but this couple can be very happy if they find key ideas and goals to share. The organised Virgo will appreciate the Saturn ruled part of Aquarius that represents structure and order but less so their rebellious Uranus side who enjoys throwing the rulebook out. Airy Aquarius and Mercury ruled Virgo are both free thinkers and should be good at allowing each other room to breathe in the relationship which both parties will value in their partner. Optimistic Aquarius and pragmatic Virgo will need to find a shared ambition to balance out their stark differences.

LIBRA: COMPATIBILITY 5/5

When these two Air signs of Aquarius and Libra
fall in love, it can be a whirlwind romance. Ruled by
Venus and Uranus, this may well be a rebellious or
radical type of love. Libra is a cardinal sign and is
quick to come up with ideas and Aquarian's mode is
fixed so makes an ideal partner to actualise their Libra
lover's plans; teamwork really is dreamwork for this
outgoing positive couple. The ideals of an Aquarius
paired with Libra's righteousness can form a couple
that will break down boundaries and create their own
rules to make their ideal future.

SCORPIO: COMPATIBILITY 1/5

Mysterious Scorpio and unique Aquarius may well
find themselves attracted to one another, but the
Scorpion and Water Bearer may need to work hard
to keep their relationship off the rocks. Positive
Aquarians are outgoing, and socialising in their
communities is important but this is different for
introverted Scorpios who tend to have a small and
intimate circle of friends. Their modes are both fixed
which means they can be resistant to changing their
contrasting outlooks. If stable Scorpio can embrace
this Air sign's free spirited nature and rational
Aquarius can provide the intimacy that Scorpio needs,
then these two could find their happiness.

SAGITTARIUS: COMPATIBILITY 4/5

Placed two apart on the zodiac calendar, the positive
energies of an Aquarian and Sagittarian can be a
complimentary and exciting love match. The thrilling
ideas of a Sagittarius combined with Aquarian's
independent thinking can mean that these stimulating
spouses will have plenty to talk about. The Fire in
Sagittarius brings an enthusiastic energy to the
relationship and the fixed mode of Aquarius can help
provide a focus to their ideas and bring them into fruition.
Communal minded Aquarius and sociable Sagittarius will
likely be at the heart of their shared communities and
bring great meaning to each other's lives.

CAPRICORN: COMPATIBILITY 1/5

Both ruled by Saturn, Capricorns and Aquarians will
usually have a good understanding of the rules of love,
however, Aquarians are co-ruled by Uranus so may
rebel against the traditions that most Capricorns value.
A Capricorn and an Aquarius can both be extremely
independent people which may be what attracts them
to one another, and as a creative couple they can really
bring out the best in each other. This is a union of
strong personalities and beliefs that may struggle to
find common ground due to their opposite negative
and positive energies, although their differences and
determination could be their success.

AQUARIUS: COMPATIBILITY 3/5

When two Air signs fall in love, it is usually a kindred
meeting of the minds, but they should remember to
share their hearts too. What may have first started as a
friendship, the relationship of two Aquarians is unlikely
to be stuck in the mud with both parties interested in
progressing their feelings further. As a couple they may
challenge the norm and their love can certainly seem
radical to outsiders. Both individuals can be guilty of
being stubborn or superior so should try loosening up
their fixed attitudes. If these two share the same vision
their future can be thought provoking and innovative.

PISCES: COMPATIBILITY 2/5

Two very giving signs such as Pisces and Aquarius
could happily give themselves to each other in
love. Whilst an Air and Water sign may struggle to
understand one another, an Aquarian's intellect
combined with a Piscean's compassion can form a
relationship that speaks to both the heart and head if
flexibility and patience is practised by the pair. A fixed
and mutable mode can be a complimentary match, so
long as Aquarians don't try to bend the will of their
accommodating Piscean partner. The bond that these
two can share when at its best can be sincere and
spiritually liberating.

FAMILY AND FRIENDS

Having a friend in Aquarius is surely having a friend for life. Whether this faithful sign has seen their chums last week or last year, these friendly souls will happily pick up where they last left off. Despite their likeable positive natures, their original and unconventional thoughts can at times make it hard for this sign to relate to their family and friends. Whether the loved ones of an Aquarius believe in the same things as them or not, surrounding themselves with open-minded people who will listen to their vast and sometimes controversial ideas will help this sign form bonds. Befriending a mutable sign like a Piscean or Sagittarian who will usually welcome a change of perspective could help Aquarians air their ideas freely and without judgment. For an intellectual chat or non-stop gossip, Air signs like Libra and Gemini will always be happy to exchange ideas and chat endlessly with their Aquarian friend. Born in the eleventh house of friendship and community, being a member of a club or society is where Aquarians can feel most at home. There can be a secret side to Aquarius, some will certainly value their privacy, so perhaps a secret society or hanging out in a bar off the beaten track will be where to find this sign catching up with friends.

Aquarius' uniqueness could extend to their choice of home as this sign may find that they do not feel comfortable in a traditional setting such as a two-up two-down terraced house. Instead, they may feel more at home in a converted barn or church, or whatever perhaps best suits their one-off personality. Inside an Aquarian's home, their choice of interior is likely to continue to reflect their utterly unique personality; think eclectic and antique trinkets rather than Swedish flat pack furniture. Wherever this nomadic character decides to settle, building a social network will be key to them and they will no doubt be a positive pillar in their community. Symbolised by the Water Bearer, Aquarians are intent on making their community flourish and their giving and friendly ways will usually have them working in a team for the greater good. This Water Bearer might be found raising money for their local watering hole or at the local council meeting speaking their mind on how to best improve their local area for the benefit of everyone.

When it comes to the family of an Aquarian, they will always try to work as a team. Born in the eleventh house where teamwork is key, Aquarians may be the one that encourages each member of the family to vocalise their thoughts and have a vital input into the way they function as a household. As with their own life, Aquarians may favour an alternative path for their children also. Home schooling may be an Aquarian's preference if they find that their local schools are too traditional for their liking. Aquarians will not want their children to miss out on group activities so enrolling their child in sports or other social clubs could be a priority. However, as with any functional community, the voice of everyone will be heard in an Aquarian's home and their children may have the deciding vote or at least a valid input.

MONEY AND CAREERS

Being a certain star sign will not dictate the type of career that you have, although the characteristics that fall under each sign could help you identify the areas in which you could potentially thrive. Conversely, to succeed in the workplace, it is just as important to understand what you are good at as it is to know what you are less brilliant at so that you can see the areas in which you will need to perhaps work harder to achieve your career and financial goals.

When it comes to money, Aquarians are usually far more interested in the exchange of ideas than of cash. If an Aquarian is money focused it will generally be because they want to help their community in some way. To their friends and family, Aquarius is known for their seemingly endless generosity and this Water Bearer will come to parties with their arms full of wine and treats for all. This sign is normally fixated on doing things for the benefit of their fellow human so raising funds for a local charity or donating their money to help restore a nearby youth hostel are the types of projects that this giving sign may like to spend their money on. Aquarians won't typically be satisfied with donating just their money to the good of the community and may find that their vocation is working as a social worker or in another public sector where they believe they can best serve their community and make a difference, like human rights lawyer Amal Clooney, equal rights campaigner Rosa Parks or suffragette Susan B. Anthony. Aquarians want to make their communities better places and make a difference for everyone.

As an Air sign, a career that stretches their mind should be well suited to an Aquarian. This futuristic sign could be set on inventing the next world changing invention, theory, or technological advancement like Aquarians Thomas Edison or Charles Darwin. So innovative and outspoken is this sign that people are certainly inclined to listen to them in the workplace, even if their colleagues don't quite agree with their unique perspective. With Saturn by their side, Aquarians will usually be highly devoted to their work responsibilities and can be some of the most reliable and hard-working of signs. The authority given to this sign by Saturn could help Aquarians become a highly successful team manager or commanding boss of their own company, like Duncan Bannatyne. Their positive energy can be a stimulating force in the office and born in the eleventh house makes them both inspiring leaders and energetic team players – look at famous Aquarians Abraham Lincoln or Franklin D. Roosevelt to see how this sign can take charge and inspire people even in the trickiest of situations.

Whilst you can't always choose who you work with, it can be advantageous to learn about colleagues' key characteristics through their star signs to try and work out the best ways of working with them.

Feeling the influence of radical Uranus can make it
hard for Aquarians to follow someone else's rules,
so their relationships with managers and bosses
could be challenging at times if they do not share the
same ethos. Born in the first house that represents
the self, Aries could be a colleague that jars with the
community minded Aquarius, whilst fellow Air sign
Libra could be the pioneering ideas seeking boss that
gels well with Aquarius.

HEALTH AND WELLBEING

· · · · · · · · · · · · · · · · · ·

Another way in which this Air sign can help clear their mind is by making sure that their environments are both peaceful and functional. Ensuring that their element of Air and energy can flow freely throughout their household may be an Aquarian's priority so introducing the Chinese practice of feng shui into their home and office space could help restore some harmony.

Associated with blood circulation, an adrenaline fuelled sport that gets an Aquarian's blood pumping could be how this energetic sign likes to stay fit and healthy. This alternative Air sign might literally be in their element taking on daring sports like base jumping or paragliding. Or if heights aren't an Aquarian's thing, skiing or snowboarding off piste somewhere a little different in the world might be more suited to this unconventional sign. After an active day on the slopes, a little *après ski* sauna will no doubt be where Aquarians make a beeline for in order to give their tired muscles and blood circulation that extra boost.

Having a healthy cholesterol level is essential for everyone wanting to live a long and healthy life, but it may be something that this sign is more keenly aware of to keep their associated body system of blood circulation thriving. Eating healthily is a great way to feel healthier and a proven way to naturally lower a high cholesterol, so if this is a concern for any star sign, reducing their intake of foods that are high in saturated fats such as red meat and cheese is always a good place to start. Making a few adjustments to diet, such as ordering the tuna steak rather than the beef, should boost the body with healthier omega three fats and have any sign, Aquarius included, feeling much healthier. Aquarians should try not being a total stranger to their local GP, even if they prefer to practise alternative home remedies to battle the flu rather than get their annual jab, and always seek professional guidance if they have concerns about their health.

Mental health should be tended to just as readily as physical health and, as for any Air sign, having a happy and clear mind is essential to an Aquarian's wellbeing. If an Aquarian's head is feeling clogged up with stress or worries, their usually innovative and free flowing ideas can feel blocked which can compound an Air sign's anxiety. Identifying the root of the problem could be the first step as the cause of anxiety may or may not be obvious. By tackling issues candidly, an Aquarian can then plan the most practical route to a happy solution, which could include turning to their beloved community, be it a neighbour or sibling, and asking for help.

Aquarius

· · · · · · · · · · · · · · · · ·

2020
DIARY PAGES

JANUARY

. . . .

Wednesday 1st
Happy New Year Aquarius. Just coming out of 2019
you may have high hopes for 2020. Some of the stories
you have been through will find their end and you
can prepare for the new ones to begin. You will need
perseverance and discipline, but in the end, you can
make good use of your uniqueness.

Thursday 2nd
So much is going on in your subconscious you do lots
of work at an internal level. With Mercury and Jupiter
in combination, it can be like something is finally
dawning upon you. Sit with whatever comes up from
your subconscious, note down everything that pops
into your mind.

Friday 3rd
This is an excellent day for communicating, and you
will connect in various ways. With Mars on the edge of
your area of career and legacy, it is likely that you try to
put the finishing touches to a project and with Mercury
on the south node, you come across a restriction that is
inside yourself.

Saturday 4th

Mars enters your area of friends, community and tribe. It is pleasant energy for you to have as you like to connect with various people, love to bring them all together, love to socialise and be of service. You will love this transit, and it won't have a dull moment.

Sunday 5th

Home sweet home, as the Moon enters Taurus and with this your area of home and family. You will likely have a fantastic time connecting with your family members and just enjoy the day. It is also an excellent day to have some Me-time as it is easier for you to reflect when you are comfortable.

Monday 6th

In the safety of your home you feel grounded enough to do the inner work, and with Saturn and Pluto both in your 12th house, there is lots of reconditioning and restructuring going on. It is not an easy task, but to be innovative and anchor in the new ground, you first have to deal with the old.

Tuesday 7th

Saturn and Pluto are merging their powers. It is all about your conditioning, your past, the structures around you and the restrictions you have faced so far. There is an act of liberation and empowerment going on. While you are in this process nothing comes easy, but it carries the promise of the new, and that keeps you going.

Wednesday 8th

Venus, the planet of love, beauty and harmony, is
currently in your sign, so this adds to your charm,
and you might feel even more appreciation from your
surroundings. Too much of that is hard to handle for
you, but as long as it doesn't go too deep, you like to
flirt around.

Thursday 9th

There is fantastic energy today, and you could be in a
very creative mood. With the Moon connecting to Venus
you can easily delight, and have just the right words
at hand. It would be easy to pick someone up if that is
what you desire. Most likely you just want to play.

Friday 10th

Happy Full Moon Lunar Eclipse in your area of
everyday life. Mercury is firmly connected in this one,
as it is in the arms of the Sun. This Moon asks you to
get a grip on your emotions and to express them daily,
instead of hiding them behind closed doors and even
from yourself.

Saturday 11th

Uranus is your planetary ruler, and it goes direct today!
That means the universe's clock creates a lot of forward
momentum now and once you have cleared some of
the old ways, the new ground can be covered. For you,
this happens in your home and family sector, which at
times can become challenging.

Sunday 12th

Two powerful influences at once. The Moon comes into your area of relationships; an area where you are asked to stay true to yourself and follow your heart. Meanwhile Mercury joins the Saturn-Pluto hug. All this translates as some transformative changes being brought into your consciousness. You had better make some diary entries.

Monday 13th

The Sun now also joins Saturn and Pluto, so you will likely have a moment in which you realise that the old is indeed outdated and the old structures no longer work. Venus is on her final day in your sign, so if you wish to go out and let your charm play then you can.

Tuesday 14th

Venus will now beautify your area of possessions, self-worth and material things. She loves this area, so if you are considering buying things or making investments this is undoubtedly a good time. Interestingly enough, the Moon is in the field of shared resources so find what is already available before you go to the counter.

Wednesday 15th

Today's energy can feel a little heavy or at least a little too real for your liking. It is at least good to get lots of stuff done and get your schedule ready. Schedules may seem a little boring, but in the end, they help you to ground yourself and not fly off the track. They can become essential resources to use.

Thursday 16th

Take at least a moment today to reflect on your inner processes. This can be a diary entry, writing down keywords, thoughts, whatever is coming up for you. It is worthwhile for you to capture your thoughts because they are so fast and diverse, some of them could get lost along with their potential.

Friday 17th

Mercury, the messenger, is moving into your sign. This is an excellent place for innovative thoughts, creative genius and ideas that can be ahead of their time. A great exercise would be to have a whiteboard, paper or booklet where you note down all the keywords and brainwaves that come to you, no matter how irrelevant they seem to be.

Saturday 18th

The messenger is in discussion with your planetary guide Uranus. Uranus wants to break new ground but in an area that you would prefer to keep as it is. So when you recognise some of the necessary changes, you are likely to feel resistance. Alas, this won't make it easier.

Sunday 19th

The Moon in Scorpio connects you to your legacy and vocation and actually this is the area where you love to go deep. You are currently working on changing your conditioning to become the revolutionary you intend to be. Today might have an event in store that acts as a stepping stone.

Monday 20th

Moon into Sagittarius and Sun into Aquarius. Funny they both end on I-us. These bring incredible energy for you to focus on community, to share, explore, exchange and dream big. Today is filled with activity and meetings, and you will thrive on the variety that this brings.

Tuesday 21st

With the Sun now in your sign, your birthday season begins. So happy birthday to all Aquarians! You have the opportunity to focus on your self-expression, your persona and the mask you are wearing. Use this opportunity to focus on your strengths and what you want this new year to hold.

Wednesday 22nd

The Moon in Capricorn is likely to be a more reflective time for you, or one in which you try and meet your obligations. The sense of responsibility is great but try not to be so hard on yourself. It is possible that your energy feels a little flat so take a rest when needed.

Thursday 23rd

Get ready, the universe is going to throw you a curve ball today. The Sun and Uranus are in a debate, and it could invoke some rebellious feelings inside you. Your sense of emotional security could be shaken up or you might feel like you need to break out of this game.

Friday 24th

Happy New Moon in Aquarius. It is one of the most important ones for you, as it is in your sign. It is a good time for all intentions regarding your self-development, and to accept and love your uniqueness. It is essential to know your core and nurture it before you set out to save the world.

Saturday 25th

This is likely to be a very active day. You will be out and about, a coffee here, some small talk there, meeting a bunch of people for afternoon tea and then out all night dancing. If life is vibrant, you feel alive and kicking. Dance it out!

Sunday 26th

You can feel in total alignment today as your feelings and your mind are on the same page so to speak. It is a fantastic day for abstract thoughts and great concepts as you are a little detached. Today you are not much into togetherness at least not on an intimate level.

Monday 27th

Create some space for meditating and connecting spiritually. The Moon enters Pisces and Venus joins Neptune. This is an energy of higher love, imagination and intuition. Oneness with all. You can tap into that field when you quiet your mind. Being near water might also help.

Tuesday 28th

The universal love energy continues to flow, and you can want to detach from reality and drift away. Delay appointments and decisions that need clarity. Watch a movie or read a book to enter other worlds. Yoga is great because it connects the spiritual with the physical.

Wednesday 29th

A busy day ahead with lots of messages and questions incoming. It will likely stir your curiosity and inspire you to the max. Have your notebook and a pencil handy as there are so many thoughts in your head that you should try to note at least some keywords. Shut down your phone and notifications if it is getting too much.

Thursday 30th

You might come across something today that gives you an icky or edgy feeling. It could be a question asked that literally questions your belief structure or is in conflict with your conditioning. Another option is it becomes evident that your day-to-day life does not feel nurturing to you.

Friday 31st

More inspirational sparks fly your way but can you handle them? It is not easy to pull down the tower of restrictions, and you can sometimes try to avoid getting to the core of things. You are asked to act on your inner truth and tear down those walls for good.

FEBRUARY

....

Saturday 1st

What about a family weekend, with hardly any
interruptions? You can either love or hate today's energy.
It can play out in a comforting and stabilising way, but it
could also feel a little boring and slow to you. You can't
run around at high speed all the time, can you?

Sunday 2nd

There are some beautiful aspects today. Venus in a lovely
connection to Pluto can help you manifest your deepest
desire in a fair and selfless way, and the Moon connects to
Jupiter to expand your sense of inner and outer security.
The Moon also asks you to act on your intentions.

Monday 3rd

The start of the week can feel like a rocket launching.
So much energy is available to you, your mind is sharp
and is sparking genius. You are highly creative and love
to express yourself. To make the best out of this energy,
ground thoroughly through physical activity, eating well
or taking long deep breaths.

Tuesday 4th

Mercury is now moving into Pisces, which might feel a little confusing or challenging for you because the energy is so different from your own. It is an excellent opportunity to train your intuition and deepen a spiritual praxis that involves the body, perhaps through yoga, tai chi or qi gong.

Wednesday 5th

Spark your creativity and spark it with friends. You will find many ways to express yourself and connect to a community be it virtually or in the real world. It is necessary to find a way to integrate your actions within a tribe. Mercury and Uranus connect and create an underlying sense of peace.

Thursday 6th

You are very focused on your daily routine and health today. It is vital that your habits create a feeling of nourishment and that you take good care of yourself. Despite going for trends like smoothies or superfoods, just find what feels best for you and eat regularly as it also helps you to ground.

Friday 7th

Venus is on her final day in Pisces, which might give some emotional intensity while the Moon is trying to find balance and harmony with all those planets in Capricorn. You might find yourself moody and exhausted while trying to follow all impulses. Have a pause, whenever necessary.

Saturday 8th

Lots of Fire energy is available today with the Moon and Venus entering into Fire signs. You thrive on this energy. It a great day to have funny or loving conversations and to have some time for togetherness. You might have an idea how to improve your day today that includes your partner.

Sunday 9th

Happy Full Moon in Leo! This moon illuminates your one-to-one relationships and the love in your life. It is about love in general and differentiating between your needs and wants and the demands of others. You have a big heart Aquarius, listen carefully to what it is whispering to you right now.

Monday 10th

A secret from your past could be revealed today. There might be a tendency to try and analyse it too closely, but it is highly questionable if that approach is constructive. It might be helpful for you to release structures you used to maintain. Try to leave the logic aside and discover how it makes you feel.

Tuesday 11th

It is helpful to consider all the resources available to you while you reinvent your inner world. It could also be possible that the precious resources you have seem to bind you to the past and the structures you grew up in. There is no general wrong or right here. Stay observant.

Wednesday 12th

Once again the energy feels a little tense. Today you are trying to make everything right and please everyone. This is in conflict with your own emotional security. It is honourable to take everyone's opinion into consideration, but you need to find your dreams and visions and follow them as well.

Thursday 13th

You could wish yourself far away today, travelling around the globe and meeting lots of different people. Nothing speaks against that, but you need to realise that you can never escape yourself no matter how far away you wander. There will always be battles you need to fight within yourself.

Friday 14th

Happy Valentine's day! The Moon is in your area of work and vocation so there can be a tendency to throw yourself into action and miss out on that cliché Valentine's dinner. It's nothing that you would really care about, but should your honey fail to mark the day you will feel offended anyhow.

Saturday 15th

You have no clue what is going on and your mind
seems to play tricks on you. That is not really the case,
but your logical and detached approach is finally not
working. Like it or not, your emotions need a voice and
your intuitive understanding can be high if you just
dare to tune in.

Sunday 16th

Mars moves into Capricorn and adds energy to your area
of self-reflection. Any inner work that you have avoided
so far will be done during this transit, as Mars is at its
most determined and willing to climb the mountain. You
will see yourself pushing through your subconscious
and bringing up a variety of themes.

Monday 17th

Mercury starts its retrograde motion so now there is
only a little chance left that brooding will aid you.
Choose to dream, to imagine and dwell in fantasies.
Try to remember your dream and note down what you
remember. Train your intuition and allow the logic to
rest for a moment.

Tuesday 18th

Jupiter is in a lovely connection to Neptune, and together
they can dissolve and cross any boundary. It is a day to
dream more significantly than ever before. Stay away
from any mind-altering substances as that would be just
too much. And too much of a good thing is a bad thing.

Wednesday 19th

The Sun enters Pisces and connects to the Moon in a
flowing conversation. It is a fantastic day to retreat and
meditate or do yoga. Flowing water can help you to
ground this energy even more, so if you have the chance,
go for a walk by the riverside, or listen to water sounds.

Thursday 20th

It is likely you still feel a little far away from outside world
demands, as you have many transforming processes going
on inside. Take as much time as possible for yourself and
practise stillness. It can be hard to sit with yourself, but
you need to do it. Try guided meditations.

Friday 21st

Mars connects to Uranus, and when these two
combine the results can be electric. This could be a
sudden insight regarding your home and family life
or maybe someone literally coming unexpectedly to
your door. It is likely to be a welcome interruption no
matter how it shows up.

Saturday 22nd

The Moon is in your sign, and you can make great
connections today. Your charm is emphasised, and
you want to appear different. Your sense of freedom
is enhanced, and it will be better if you have no
obligations. Otherwise, you will want to do just the most
necessary tasks and be out and about having fun.

Sunday 23rd

Happy New Moon in Pisces. There is a strong focus on imagination, compassion and dreams as well as material things and physical activity. It is an excellent time to set intentions about how to anchor your fantasies and decide what is of value. You could also start to support a charity.

Monday 24th

Venus is in a debate with Jupiter but these two like each other so much that discussion will only help you out. This discussion might be about the right questions to ask and to choose your words wisely. You can be a little too blunt or say too much. Sometimes silence is golden.

Tuesday 25th

Mars sits right on top of the south node which can help you to make good use of the skillset you have, or it asks you to let go of something that is no longer serving you. Use your intuition to figure out what it is.

Wednesday 26th

Mercury, the messenger, is *Cazimi*, in the heart of the Sun. Here he receives instructions to move further along his path. You will likely gain some insight about how to make your intuition more tangible. Allow some time for this information to sink in. You might need to access this intuitively.

Thursday 27th

Another busy day ahead and so many impulses that want to be explored. You can be a little moody and overwhelmed by this energy. Do one thing at a time, avoid distractions and multi-tasking. Take some time to write down your thoughts, otherwise your mind could spin in circles.

Friday 28th

Moon in Taurus for a Friday is quite lovely as it will likely allow you to spend some time with your family. The energy is peaceful, and even you might feel like putting on comfy clothes and staying at home to watch a movie. The movie itself can be off-beat and exciting.

Saturday 29th

Venus is in a debate with Pluto, the great transformer and destructor. You might feel like you just cannot continue to communicate as usual. Power struggles can arise. Beware believing you know best and deserve to have the upper hand. Focus on your values of equality and fairness.

MARCH

················

Sunday 1st

It is a silent and comfortable Sunday that allows you
to recharge your batteries. Enjoy a family breakfast,
sing with your rubber duck in the tub or lie on the
ground and dwell on your thoughts. In those times of
rest, exciting ideas and thoughts can arise. So that is an
excellent reason to unwind, isn't it?

Monday 2nd

A perfect start into this new week with your creativity
level at its peak. You will have lots of inspiring
conversations, and your curiosity might lead you to new
discoveries. You feel a variety of impulses, but some of
them are just chit-chat and gossip. Try to differentiate.

Tuesday 3rd

What are you going to do with these new impulses?
You might not have a clue, as your mind is still
working differently and you don't know how to
combine intuition and logic. In the world of dream and
imagination, not everything has to be taken literally.
Think of metaphors.

Wednesday 4th

Some useful energy is aiding you to move forward with your project. Begin the day with a morning routine and prep your meals. Mercury comes back into your sign, so it is still in a rethinking, re-evaluating process but you can make more sense out of everything, and something might click soon.

Thursday 5th

Venus comes into your area of home and family, a place where she is super powerful. This transit can bring the desire to beautify your home, get some high-class items for decoration, do some gardening or indulge in fantastic food. The way you relate to your family will also be part of it.

Friday 6th

How much is Me-time already integrated into your everyday life? You sometimes have a hard time being by yourself but these times are incredibly important for your health. Reserve a spot for yourself every single day, maybe even put it into your calendar if it assists you to commit.

Saturday 7th

Relationships are in focus, and you surely don't want to waste this energy. You love to receive a little admiration from your partner, so you do your best to shine in your best colours. Leave the show aside and tune into your heart and you will find your partner smiling back at you with sparkling delight in their eyes.

Sunday 8th

Today's energy is peculiar! On the one hand, it is highly romantic and perfect to experience some tenderness, but you could easily feel restless and trapped. You need to feel free and a workaround for today might be to travel with your partner to combine these two very different needs.

Monday 9th

Happy Full Moon in Virgo. This Full Moon illuminates the depth of your relationships and how much space you allow for sensual and sexual experiences. It is hard for you to let go and surrender, but when you are in your head all the time you miss the pleasure component completely.

Tuesday 10th

Mercury has done enough re-evaluating, rethinking and reconsidering and is moving forward again. He will spend some more days in your sign so you can get your head around some of the things that have seemed foggy for some time. Look at the themes that have occupied you since the beginning of February.

Wednesday 11th

The next two weeks will likely feel very intense for you. Saturn is on its final degree in Capricorn, and it is demanding that you get the message. This is happening in your area of subconscious and inner life. Grind your teeth and keep doing the inner work.

Thursday 12th

Your focus is on career and legacy matters, and you are giving everything you've got. You have an inner lie detector that allows you to sense when someone is trying to pull the wool over your eyes. You can tend to be a little over-protective of your boundaries. You are safe.

Friday 13th

It is probably an easy Friday when you can fulfil all the demands that are expected of you and show full responsibility. Later, when you call it a day, you can find comfort by staying at home and snuggling up in a blanket. There is a tendency to be in a workaholic mode, wanting to finish just one more thing.

Saturday 14th

A hidden power and a mystical vibe present themselves as the weekend begins. Take some time to get out in nature, listen to the birds heralding spring and see the daffodils reaching their heads towards the sun. There is something brewing, but you cannot grasp it. Find time for meditation and yoga.

Sunday 15th

Conversations with your friends can help you to connect with your inner power and to get conscious of some of the paradigms you are still embedded in. You can feel grateful to know such a variety of people: for every mood there is one to connect to, and as different as they are, they all value your thoughts.

Monday 16th

Time to get the imaginative and intuitive thinking going again. Mercury is back in Pisces now, moving forward and getting ready to go all the way. Soon you will be able to reap the rewards of your more in-depth explorations, tune into your intuition and surrender to not knowing.

Tuesday 17th

Uranus is in a harmonious conversation with the lunar nodes, or destiny. As your planetary guide, what he is doing is vitally important for you. You can expect some wake-up calls and liberating actions but they won't be disturbing or shocking. Instead they leave you a feeling of freedom.

Wednesday 18th

A busy day, especially on an internal level. Be easy on yourself today and maybe wear a shirt that is labelled: 'caution could implode easily.' Dare to be moody and don't repress all the emotions rising to the surface. Do some breath work and ground thoroughly.

Thursday 19th

Goodness, gracious you really do feel a sense of relief as the Moon shifts into your sign and allows you to detach. It takes a lot of pressure from you, and you will feel a bit more like yourself. Go for some excitement and weirdness today, weirdness meaning just something unusual that no one is expecting.

Friday 20th

Happy Spring Equinox! Day and night are equal today with the Sun about to beat the night. Mars connects to Jupiter, so powerful things are brewing in your subconscious and you can expect a good revelation soon. The Sun enters your house of communication and learning which promises excitement ahead.

Saturday 21st

The Moon enters Pisces and buffers a bit of the exciting energy, it also connects to Mercury so you will find your emotions and mind in alignment and you will have an easy time trusting your intuition, which for you is a big deal. Watch your dreams as there could be messages coming in.

Sunday 22nd

Mark your calendar, this is a special day. Saturn, the planet of manifestation, time, cycles and discipline is leaving Capricorn and enters your sign. It is in and of itself a fascinating transit, and that goes double for you. With Saturn here, you receive the stamina to anchor in the new. It is dipping toes for now, but powerful nevertheless.   .

Monday 23rd

Mars meets Pluto today, and this signifies power. With the Sun currently in Aries watch your tongue and beware not to blurt out what you might regret later. It is your actions aligning to your inner core, and that is incredibly powerful. You most likely need to release this energy somehow. Running around the block?

Tuesday 24th

Happy New Moon in Aries, this is a powerhouse of a New Moon. Ready to set you up for a new way of communicating and new learnings. Listen to your gut to figure out where to focus and stay observant as there are some important things about to happen.

Wednesday 25th

There is not a dull moment, is there? Today's energy still has you fully engaged and trying to connect all the dots and open loops. You will likely feel very alive and powerful. Take care not to exhaust yourself, take breaks and try to find some sleep early.

Thursday 26th

It is another intense day, as the Moon is making hard connections to almost everything today. So if you feel a little restless, don't fall into despair. At least stuff is going on. Take a much-needed rest during the day and try to get out in nature.

Friday 27th

Friday is here and compared to the marathon the week
has been so far, today offers unexpected peace and
calmness. It could almost feel a little annoying. But the
weekend is approaching, and as the sun is setting, you
might go out and have a fancy dinner.

Saturday 28th

Venus is in a fluid connection to Jupiter which is about
good fortune and expansion in general. This can bring a
tendency to overindulge, so keep an eye on that. Today
would be perfect to retreat in a spa, relax and feel the
love flowing through the universe.

Sunday 29th

You can't wait to get up and connect and might have
written 20 messages even before breakfast. You want to
have some fun today and don't mind it if it's superficial.
As long as it is different and amusing, it is good. If you
get bored, you are gone faster than a flash.

Monday 30th

Today is exciting. Mercury is finally out of shadow which
means he will not cover new areas, and you might be
done with something that started in early February.
Simultaneously, Mars, the planet of action, is finishing
in Capricorn and entering your sign, supporting you to
take action on your behalf.

Tuesday 31st

Ah wait, Saturn is waiting at the doorstep telling Mars to remain responsible before unleashing all its power and going for your cause. After all, you have a mission and want to reform the world. So don't consider this an invitation to an ego-trip. This would surely backfire.

APRIL

. . . .

Wednesday 1st

The current energy supports your ability to nurture and take good care of yourself. Daily routines, even minor ones, go a long way. You might want to integrate a new habit but can't decide which one to choose. Let your intuition and gut feeling help you decide.

Thursday 2nd

There is lots of fire in the air, and you can try and channel this energy in your relationship, or there could be a tendency to be a drama queen or king. You do want some special attention, but many paths lead to Rome.

Friday 3rd

Venus, planet of love and beauty, is moving into Gemini, which for you means a particular emphasis on self-love, joy, fun, children and self-expression. She will stay for a long while as she is about to transform herself and allow you to reinvent yourself on a creative level.

Saturday 4th

Saturn seems to be on a mission to set everyone straight from the beginning and connects harmoniously to Venus. How you revolutionise your self-expression is vital for your future. With Mercury in conjunction with Neptune, you can use art to express and reveal hidden messages. Your dreams might be vivid so get that notebook handy.

Sunday 5th

Today you want to get to the bottom of things and figure out what is real. There is a good chance you will be successful as Jupiter and Pluto conjoin for the first time. This could result in great self-empowerment or self-trust rising from deep within.

Monday 6th

The Moon is now in a harmonious connection to the Jupiter-Pluto meeting, so emotions will be super vibrant and you might get a brand new idea about how to use resources for your benefit. You have the power to get things started and be ahead of your time.

Tuesday 7th

The vision of real equality and justice is something you hold high. In this world, it is not always easy to achieve, especially not if you want to please others. In family circles it can be challenging to be truly yourself, but honestly, you have no chance if you don't show your true colours.

Wednesday 8th

Happy Full Moon in Libra! This is all about your vision
and its expansion for the highest good. It is a great time
to have a look at what your visions are. What have you
already manifested, what ideas are outdated and need
to make room for some others? It is also an invitation to
dream of your personal utopia.

Thursday 9th

The Scorpio Moon is challenging you to stand in your
own truth. There is no other way for you to be if you want
to follow your vocation. You need to be all in, to focus
your energy. You might feel pressured to act while your
family could demand your attention. Listen to your heart.

Friday 10th

Venus is now entering her shadow phase. That
means she will come back to that place and it also
means everything that is currently going on for you
related to creativity, self-love and expression or your
children is likely to be revisited. There is a need for a
metamorphosis.

Saturday 11th

Oh, happy day! Two planetary shifts happen in your
favour. First of all, the Moon is in Sagittarius which
highlights your need and ability to connect with your
friendship and social groups of all kinds, and second,
Mercury finishes in Pisces and enters Aries which brings
your wit to new heights.

Sunday 12th

Mercury connects to Saturn, so you can bet there is lots of prep-work going on for a significant shift. This will help you to figure out what you need to do. Likely you will feel relieved to be free from some unfocused energy and can now use your mind to its full capacity.

Monday 13th

This is the final time that the Moon enters Capricorn with the south node here. A chapter is about to end. Take some time for yourself and note down everything you want to leave behind and also what skills you want to take with you and how you want to use them in a new way.

Tuesday 14th

The third-quarter Moon indicates a crisis in consciousness. How can you reap the fruits of your inner work and show up full of self-esteem and as a real reformer in your immediate community? You need to start somewhere, and your task is to get your message across. Start locally.

Wednesday 15th

Sun-Jupiter days are usually excellent, but they are in dispute with each other so boundaries might be crossed and rules might be broken. You can find yourself going too far today and need to bear the consequences. It is unlikely that this is going to be super bad. But possibly unnecessary.

Thursday 16th

The Moon is in your sign and in a harmonious connection to Venus. You thrive on unique ideas which seem to come to you in an unstoppable flow. Dare to experiment in how you express them and allow your curiosity to guide you. Set all hesitations aside.

Friday 17th

Use your resources Aquarius and don't forget that imagination is a resource you can tap into quickly. To access it, put it out there in reality. There is no use in moving it from brain cell to brain cell. You need to make it accessible so that you can share it with others.

Saturday 18th

Another day to be creative and get your message out in various ways. The challenge is to remain focused on the task at hand. You can quickly become scattered and finish none of the initiatives you started. Write new ideas down but stick with the one you started to work on.

Sunday 19th

The Sun moves into Taurus and adds some stamina and stability. This also connects to your home and family life but also to your roots and the feeling of being rooted. With strong roots, you can achieve almost anything so use this transit to figure out how you can ground yourself.

Monday 20th

The Sun connects to the north node as if to give you a
broad hint. Setting up a nourishing routine and creating
eating habits should help you to root and sustain your
energy. Connecting to your emotions can be vital too.
You become detached and aloof all too easily, not only
from others but from your own feelings.

Tuesday 21st

The Aries Moon can connect to both Venus and Mars
and support their mission with some fierce energy. You
will feel super motivated to push forward regarding your
projects and self-expression. The Sun has a discussion
with Saturn so this might pose an obstacle that needs to
be overcome. Did you do the necessary research?

Wednesday 22nd

Your energy is falling flat because the Moon is getting
into its dark phase. After all those days moving full
steam ahead, it might be a good thing to take it easy. You
become erratic when stressed. Beware you don't loose
your tongue too much, you can be a little blunt.

Thursday 23rd

Happy New Moon in Taurus. This one is about setting
new intentions regarding everything that relates to
home and family. If you are considering a move, it is an
excellent time to start searching for a new home. If you
want to renovate, start planning. Taking care of family
members is also advised.

Friday 24th

You would love to be a little lazy and just seeking physical rest and pleasure, but your mind is restless and keeps running uncontrollably. While proceeding with your work, keep yourself entertained as best as possible. If you can get some fun into your work, you can compensate for the lack of physical energy.

Saturday 25th

Caution, your mind is about to trick you. You might find yourself reacting in a subconscious pattern rigidly being adamant that you are right and know what to do. You want to be in charge and can quickly seem overbearing. Take a deep breath every time you want to burst with anger.

Sunday 26th

The Sun meets your planetary guide Uranus, which is something like a superpower moment. It is a new cycle beginning, and you should take notice of any events happening today. Keep your journal at hand. Pluto, the planet of change and transformations moves retrograde, and something could blow your mind and leave you bewildered.

Monday 27th

Mercury comes into Taurus where it works in a somehow calmer way that will allow you to take a breath. Use this chance while it lasts, this transit will still pass quickly. With the Moon coming into Cancer today it is a perfect day for relaxing, rest and good food. The only downfall is that it is Monday.

Tuesday 28th

Find the time to be a little more down to earth, Aquarius. Your day to day life is, and you invested a lot during the last eighteen month to get in touch with your emotional needs. You don't always need to save the world, sometimes it is enough to take care of yourself.

Wednesday 29th

It becomes especially important to take good care when you consider all the internal work. You have a tendency to repress the feelings that want to surface and this can hinder your growth and evolution. Allow your emotions to be, even though you cannot name them. Just feel.

Thursday 30th

The Moon moves into Leo and is in a tug of war with Saturn. This could show that someone is being a party-pooper, could that be you? You could be envious of your partner or another person that seems to receive more attention than you do. You could spin on your heel and leave the situation.

MAY

. . . .

Friday 1st

Mercury is in a warm hug with your planetary guide, Uranus! This makes fantastic and groundbreaking insights, genius ideas and sudden breakthroughs possible. Act with integrity, and this can be one of the most exciting and important days for you. Don't forget to note everything down, you don't want to lose any of it.

Saturday 2nd

You can find yourself trying to create a plan, a structure or a checklist. There is a deep need to see your idea manifested into reality. You could focus on unimportant details that seem to validate your opinion, but in truth distract you from making the crucial steps.

Sunday 3rd

Your own perfectionism can sometimes hinder you, whilst at other times it is beneficial to make the most of your resources and power by thoroughly planning. Keep in mind there is no such thing as the perfect plan because life has twist and turns, but you are flexible enough to adapt repeatedly.

Monday 4th

Mercury is *Cazimi* again and receives a message from the Sun. It is possible that you have a decision to make regarding your home. Allow some time to consider all possible options and weigh out what serves you and your family best. Clarity will come in some days.

Tuesday 5th

A new chapter begins. The nodal axis shifts from Cancer/Capricorn to Gemini/Sagittarius. For you, this means your focus for the next eighteen months is on creativity and self-expression as well as social interactions with groups and communities on and off line. Use the opportunity; it takes eighteen years for it to come back.

Wednesday 6th

With the Moon in Scorpio, you focus on career, and this can mean a tug of war with your family life. Once you are working you get drawn in so deeply that you forget to call or that you promised to be at home early. Try to find equilibrium.

Thursday 7th

Happy Full Moon in Scorpio. This Full Moon illuminates your progress regarding your vocation, career or legacy. What have you achieved so far and what is your goal for your future? What mystery do you want to dive into, which problem do you want to solve? Count all your successes.

Friday 8th

Are you ready to socialise Aquarius? Sure you are, but during the next eighteen months prepare for some shifts regarding the circles and communities you are involved with. It is also important to remember no one is always a clever clogs, not even you. Remaining humble is good advice.

Saturday 9th

Where do you want to move to Aquarius? Where is home and what does make you feel comfortable? The answer might surface from deep within. You are ready to make a shift and renew the current house in some kind of way. Whether this is indicating a move depends on your circumstances.

Sunday 10th

The energy is perfect to broaden your mind, and you can come across some beliefs that are deeply embedded inside yourself. There is an invisible line that you cannot cross somehow, but an inner feeling tells you that this what it takes to expand beyond known boundaries.

Monday 11th

Saturn has dipped his toes into the Aquarian realm and knows he has to go back and start his retrograde motion. In order to anchor in the new, a final lesson has to be learned. You might need to release some of your fears and insecurities, to be able to stand in your real power.

Tuesday 12th

Mercury entering Gemini promises you curiosity and light-hearted energy. You will be able to reason and come to logical conclusions. The downside is that your mind can be very restless and leave you sleepless. Keep your journal handy, so your brain does not need to hold all you are processing.

Wednesday 13th

Venus is moving retrograde. In this process, she is going to transform herself from evening to morning star and shine brightly in the morning sky. You will change the way you express yourself and make sure that you are seen more vividly than ever before.

Thursday 14th

Mars is now in your area of possessions and personal resources. This also deals with your self-worth. Mars here gives you the ability to manifest, but only if you go with the flow and this is the crux. Mars loves to push ahead, but that will just leave you frustrated.

Friday 15th

Welcome to Retrograde City. Now Jupiter is moving backwards trying to figure out another way to break the boundaries, unleash your inner wisdom and install your trust. The Sun is in a lovely connection to Jupiter, so there is lots of power available to make the final decision regarding your home.

Saturday 16th

The Moon is in discussion with Venus and it's a debate about intuition vs logic. You want to listen to your gut but are constantly irritated if you find no justification for it. You could use this energy if you try and express it artistically. Be open for every result, there is nothing to lose.

Sunday 17th

The Sun is trining Jupiter, which is always a very fortunate and happy connection. If you want to try the lottery, give it a chance. But it is also possible that there are unexpected opportunities knocking at your door. All you need to do is to accept them.

Monday 18th

You jump-start the week feeling super motivated and wanting to rush forward. You could be impatient when your co-workers cannot keep up with the pace you are providing. That in return can demotivate you, and you could focus on the superficial and fall for gossip. Don't waste energy this way.

Tuesday 19th

A communication could spark your fire today and provide you with lots of stimulus and fun. Just enjoy this energy and don't try to dim it down. If you are connected to children, it is a great day to spend it with them as they will love that you can keep up the pace and are as curious as themselves.

Wednesday 20th

Both luminaries shift signs today. The Moon moves into
Taurus to enhance your sense of being comfortable
while the Sun enters Gemini and joins Mercury to
sustain your creative desires. It might be difficult to find
time to rest and follow this creative wave simultaneously.

Thursday 21st

It is one of those rare days when you would like to
stay in the comfort of your home. The overall energy
is low, and you can get through the day if you take
things easy. It is the dark phase of the Moon so don't
start anything new today.

Friday 22nd

Happy New Moon in Gemini. This is one of the most
critical New Moons this year. Not only is the north node
here, but also Venus is shifting and Gemini, the sign's
ruler, is present as well. This is powerful energy. Focus
on self-love, self-expression and creativity.

Saturday 23rd

You want to act upon your intuition but it is devoid of
logic, and this can make things tricky. Your mind and
emotions demand a rational and logical approach so you
might end up taking no action at all. A week from now,
the energy is different, and you might have more clarity.

Sunday 24th

This is the first time that the Moon crosses the new
north node in Gemini and it is amplified incredibly by
this now crescent Moon. If you have not set your goals
yet or want to take your first steps in a new direction,
there is no better time to set yourself up for the next
eighteen months to come.

Monday 25th

The Moon is in Cancer now, so you take care of your
health and find yourself more in contact with your
emotions. Now all your intuitive impulses seem to
make much more sense to you, so it is possible that
you might act upon them. This is only possible if you
switch from mind to heart.

Tuesday 26th

Inner and outer nourishing, inner and outer stability.
What is safety for you? Some questions to ponder while
you try hard to rationalise your feelings. You already
know this won't work. Try to surrender and focus
inwards. Be with yourself.

Wednesday 27th

Some Fire is in the house with the Moon coming into Leo. Lots of Air energy is available and allows this Leo Fire to burn bright. You and your partner will be able to connect passionately. Just beware those discussions could also heat up quickly and at some point, it is better to stop talking.

Thursday 28th

It was a fast transit for Mercury wearing his seven-league boots. He will take them off here in Cancer and stay a little longer, or in Mercury's terms ages. It gives you an excellent opportunity to deal with your emotions and to be honest, which is highly necessary.

Friday 29th

With the Moon in Virgo, you want to come up with a plan and stay in control. Focus this energy on your health, and you can win big time. Maybe come up with a system for buying groceries, meal prep and a weekly menu. Get out a pen and paper and go!

Saturday 30th

The energy is high to revisit some of the ideas you, hopefully, noted down and sort through them. Which ones need further investigation and research and which ones can be discarded? Focus on what is essential, and you create the opportunity to achieve a great harvest.

Sunday 31st

You might be busy all day, getting things done and checking your list. When the Moon enters Libra this afternoon, it forms a grand Air trine with Saturn and the Sun. It is loose but it is definitely energy you can fly with, and it makes it impossible for you to be a couch potato.

JUNE

. . . .

Monday 1st
How do you feel with all these internal processes going on?
It could feel like being a butterfly pupa, already knowing
you are no longer a caterpillar, but before you can start
your new existence and fly away you need to release the
entire structure that was necessary to get you here.

Tuesday 2nd
Mars and Venus are having a discussion, but it is here
to work out a solution. If you are curious enough to
try and express your creative and intuitive impulses in
a new way you could create highly interesting art and
something that lies beyond everything you ever created.

Wednesday 3rd
What is your true calling Aquarius? Today you want to
go deep emotionally. As Venus is *Cazimi*, in the heart
of the Sun, and starting a new cycle, you feel a need to
investigate your true desires further. Your emotional
reactions can be quite revealing.

Thursday 4th

The discussion between Mars and the Sun is again shining a light on making use of your intuition and following your impulses. In case you were just considering, now is the time to act. With the Moon in Sagittarius, the right people might help you to jump.

Friday 5th

Happy Full Moon in Sagittarius. This one is so revealing. A New Moon with the north node followed by a Full Moon with the south node. You wander in lots of circles, but which are the ones that are supportive to you and which ones are you really supporting? It is time to create space.

Saturday 6th

You could fall for illusion, and if you fall you fall hard when you hit reality. You could be tempted to wear some rose-coloured glasses and believe that everything is possible and all you need to do is trust and dream. Do you really want to build pipe dreams rather than reforming the world?

Sunday 7th

The Moon in Capricorn might already be the reality slap needed to get you back on track and focused on tangible results. It will take a little more, or a whole lot more to install new structures, and the first stop is still to wipe out the old.

Monday 8th

You can be tempted to test the boundaries, cross a line and figure out how much power and control you have. You will probably figure out that controlling your feelings can be useful in order to keep confidence alive, but true authenticity calls for the real deal.

Tuesday 9th

The Moon is entering your sign and you will feel great. This is also supported by all the other air energy that is still going on, so flow is guaranteed. You are filled with excitement and electricity running through your spirit that makes you literally feel the future.

Wednesday 10th

Neptune and the Sun are in a discussion and faced with very different needs. You might want to jump ahead quickly and find conclusions, but Neptune invites you to stay. Dwell and swim in your thoughts. Get a sense of what you really think to let intuition flow. Surrender.

Thursday 11th

With the Moon now in Pisces you have an easier time to tune in and act. It is like your empathy is heightened and you know exactly how to move forward. Spending time at the beach, the sea or a swimming pool and literally swimming would be a great thing to channel the energy physically.

Friday 12th

Do you fear getting lost in the beauty of a dream or illusion? It is true that this can happen, but if you never dare to dream, you can never create this concept of utopia. Dream your desires into being, but remember to look left and right when you cross the road.

Saturday 13th

The Moon, Mars and Neptune are hanging out together, and that is lots of Piscean energy. Maybe more than you can handle. But your mind is already in tune with the concept of flow. The best thing you can do is surrender and float on a boat. Grab your sunscreen and a cap and drift away.

Sunday 14th

As the Moon comes into Aries, you feel a fog dissolving. It is like you can jump up, clap your hands and are ready to go. Get your energy moving and do everything you that you delay or procrastinate over. And if you want to go out and dance, do that too!

Monday 15th

This thing called self-love, you really try to understand it today, but it is hard. How can one really feel everything and still be able to follow a routine and get everyday life done? You just want to push ahead, but if you don't recharge your batteries, you won't get far.

Tuesday 16th

A fantastic day for playfulness as well as for discoveries sparked by curiosity. Later today a home cooked meal can help you ground yourself and feel comfortable. If you want to top this, what was your favourite food when you were little? Nurture your inner child by cooking precisely that.

Wednesday 17th

You could feel a little sentimental about the changes you set up for your home. Nostalgia is nothing you are usually very drawn too, but with Uranus in your area of residence and your mind focused on your emotions lots of memories arise. But in the end: out with the old, in with the new!

Thursday 18th

Mercury, the messenger, is moving retrograde, giving you the chance to rethink, re-evaluate and re-plan. It is an excellent opportunity to reconsider which routines and daily habits are nurturing and providing safety. It is also an invitation to work with your emotions and to work through and release those that you have repressed for too long.

Friday 19th

This is not the usual Friday. Mars is in a harmonious conversation with Pluto, so you are acting towards change and evolution. Even better, the Sun is in conjunction with the north node. You want to write your message on a wall in rainbow colours and scream, "The future is coming!"

Saturday 20th

Celebrate Aquarius, celebrate! Have joy and laughter and lots of dance while you might make a night of it. What better opportunity than doing this on the shortest night, and greeting the sun rising at the Summer Solstice. This short night is as dark as it can be. Dare to face your shadow.

Sunday 21st

Happy New Moon Solar Eclipse! It sounds powerful and actually it is. It is a universal reboot after downloading a new program. A new plan for Earth and humanity. For you, it can be about setting up a new routine and setting new intentions regarding your health. And the focus on emotions is undeniable.

Monday 22nd

You feel super-sensitive today and prefer to stay with everyday tasks. You can't conquer the world all the time, can you? And congrats. Finally you allow yourself to feel and explore your sensitivity. If you can delay at least some of your duties, do so.

Tuesday 23rd

Neptune, ruling over dreams, illusion and fantasy, is moving retrograde. It is possible that this either enhances your dream life and you dream more vividly, or quite the opposite happens. Whatever the case, keep your journal ready and go to bed early. Sweet dreams, Aquarius.

Wednesday 24th

With the Moon in Leo it is time to spend some time with your darling and maybe take them out. It is not as important where you go, but rather that you can be seen. You like to stand in the spotlight or have your partner stand there and brag.

Thursday 25th

Venus retrograde is over! She is no longer to be seen in the evening sky, but rising before the Sun. She shines her light as the bright and powerful Morning star, visible in the sky also when the Sun has risen. She challenges you to shine just as bright in your creative endeavours.

Friday 26th

This is a pivotal point where you should be very aware of your actions. They can move you towards the future or throw you back to the past. Avoid reacting to situations, instead try to respond. Observe the triggers and be proud every time you don't fall for them.

Saturday 27th

This weekend starts off with lots of intensity. Mars is on the final degree of Pisces, which also marks the last degree of the zodiac. Talk about endings and new beginnings. With the Moon in a tug-of-war with Mars, this could make you wonder what is real and what is not.

Sunday 28th

With Mars entering his own sign, Aries is unleashing lots of power. There is no stopping you from pushing forward now. You are eager to learn everything that is necessary to make your visions come true. Balance is the key, otherwise you could burn yourself out quickly.

Monday 29th

You might stand in your own way. There can be a lot
of resistance inside of yourself to letting go of the
structures that have served you so well. Think back to
the butterfly. Inside the pupa, it cannot even spread its
wings, let alone know what flying will feel like.

Tuesday 30th

The Moon enters Scorpio and in this position is actually
supporting Pluto's hand in the second meeting with
Jupiter. You try to combine some very different forces.
The hidden and the known, the depth and height. There
is power in expanding not only deep but also far.

JULY

. . . .

Wednesday 1st
Mercury is back in the heart of the Sun learning a lesson about being nurtured and cared for. Once he has left there, he can tell you the story and maybe help you have an easier time understanding your emotions. You have much more time to figure this out.

Thursday 2nd
Saturn is back in Capricorn and ready to come back to your area of inner reflection to see what Jupiter and Pluto have been doing there. He gives you the opportunity to work on everything that you tried to get away with. You cannot fool Saturn, so take this chance and put the effort in.

Friday 3rd
With the Moon in Sagittarius, you love to be out and connect to your circles and tribe. The more connections, the merrier. You will be especially pleased if you can connect to a variety of people, so it doesn't become boring. Who has been the most exciting person you talked to?

Saturday 4th

The weekend is here, and you would be well advised to take some extra time for self-reflection despite hopping from party to party. With Saturn back in your sign, there is a more serious tone. Maybe go to the beach on your own or take some time to write in your journal.

Sunday 5th

Happy Full Moon in Capricorn. This Full Moon illuminates everything that is going on inside you, including all the work that you have already done, but also where you need to put more effort in. Anyway, you can pat yourself on the back and be proud of doing the work.

Monday 6th

The Moon is in your sign today and connecting to Venus, so you will most likely feel delighted. It is not a spectacular or majorly exciting day but there are some excellent vibes, and most people will be in a good mood. Sing a happy song and let your charm play.

Tuesday 7th

If you are up for a flirt, you have an easy job of it. Your charming smile and bohemian attitude attract attention. You can quickly turn someone's head, so if you just want to play make sure you let that show. You feel drawn to art recently and could make your own attempts in expressive art.

Wednesday 8th

Energy is a little edgy today as you feel impatient and pushy. You could be a little reckless, so you had better take care, especially while doing your daily chores. You could also feel a little annoyed because you cannot understand why not everybody is ready to try something new.

Thursday 9th

You could feel very empathic today which is difficult as you have a problem with drawing boundaries. You prefer to relate more rationally, and all these emotions can easily overwhelm you. Your only chance is to disconnect, and that can sometimes backfire. But for a moment you solved the problem.

Friday 10th

Your best bet today is bringing some magic and fantasy into your day. You could add a little glitter to the most straightforward conversation, go to see a movie, visit an art gallery or the museum of happiness. Focus on having some fun, and have some playtime with the children in your life.

Saturday 11th

The Moon in Aries gives you a little energy boost, even though with the Sun in Cancer, challenges can arise. What has to shift about your environment and neighbourhood to support your daily life? Are you finally making a move, maybe literally? Something is coming to fruition.

Sunday 12th

The Sun has a lovely connection to Neptune, and if you are lucky, this is a day with lots of sunshine asking you to enjoy life, eat ice-cream and be near water. Mercury is moving direct again so you can expect to implement some changes and make final decisions regarding health and routines.

Monday 13th

The Moon is coming into Taurus, combined with the Sun in Cancer. This is beautiful and nurturing energy. Maybe a little slow for your liking but if you can ease yourself into the slow pace, it can be a pleasant day. Take your loved ones out for a healthy and delicious dinner.

Tuesday 14th

Nothing better than a Sun-Jupiter day even if they are opposing each other, which means there is something askew and you need to achieve balance between the inner and the outer. How can you use your inner wisdom to improve your everyday life?

Wednesday 15th

On with the next balancing act and this one is a
little more challenging and tricky. What do you
need to transform entirely to do more satisfying and
meaningful work? How can you be of service and show
up as the humanitarian you are supposed to be?

Thursday 16th

You will likely have a restful sleep as the Moon is
finishing in Taurus. When you wake up the energy
is buzzing at least for you. You want to talk a lot and
might not be able to put your mobile aside, because
you could miss out on something important.

Friday 17th

With the Moon crossing Venus it is a day to connect to
beauty and harmony. How can you bring more beauty
into the world? Are you willing to set new trends
with your approach to self-expression and creativity?
Connect beauty to uniqueness and innovation instead
of following a known concept.

Saturday 18th

This weekend might be a little boring as nothing
unusual is happening in the outside world. Still, lots of
stuff is brewing on the inside. Wait, is this an invitation
to take time for yourself? Possibly. Other than that,
you can get lots of unfinished jobs done, which will be
weirdly satisfying.

Sunday 19th

Your mind and emotions are in perfect alignment which means there is no confusion going on in that area, and it makes it especially easy for you to get in touch with your feelings as you can somehow understand them. Draw back if you can and dive into your sea of emotions.

Monday 20th

Happy New Moon in Cancer! This is a unique New Moon happening in your area of everyday life, work and health. It is the perfect time to set up new routines and commit fully to stick with them this time. You need to figure out how to make the best use of your time.

Tuesday 21st

Leo Moon means time for love. How much time did you take for your partner recently? Show up for him or her now, and maybe say I love you with a bouquet of roses. You could also try a more passionate declaration of love. It will be well received.

Wednesday 22nd

Time to focus on your heart and let love be the only rule. The Sun ingresses Leo, and that means a spotlight on your personal relationships, business, friends and your lover. The next four weeks will have a lot in store for you, and you will be able to show your love more than you usually can.

Thursday 23rd

Are you in too deep? Try and dim down your rational approach to intimacy and hide the checklist behind your back. At least as long as your partner is demanding your attention. Afterwards get it back out, as there can be significant insights coming in and you want to make sure to focus on every detail.

Friday 24th

Another dream vs reality moment. But it passes fast. Nevertheless, other resources are somehow easier to access than your own. People are willing to support you even financially as long as they feel that what you do is serving a purpose and for the greater good. Make use of that.

Saturday 25th

This is fantastic energy for a little vacation with your partner. Where would you want to go? If you cannot leave, consider an excursion, or flipping through a travel guide or even watching a documentary. It can also be an excellent time to plan a future trip.

Sunday 26th

Your mind is tricking you by making you believe your daily life won't allow you to get out and explore the world. The truth is that, yes there are responsibilities, but why shouldn't it be possible to find balance and a mature approach to meet both needs? You are not irreplaceable at work.

Monday 27th

This is an intense day. You are focusing on your career, which might leave your partner frustrated. Venus is in a debate with Neptune about love, and this reflects your thoughts of unconditional love vs earthly conditional love. In the end with Mercury squaring up to Mars, there's nothing you can do about it.

Tuesday 28th

Today is about expansion beyond all limitations. Jupiter and Neptune connect, and both of them want to leave all restrictions behind and dissolve boundaries. It can be a day of great achievements and insights but also one where you merely overdo it on many levels. Too much of a good thing is a bad thing.

Wednesday 29th

Venus is finally leaving her shadow, which means her retrograde story is coming to a close and she enters new territory. What topic has kept you busy during the last three months? It is most likely related to creativity, self-expression, children and joy. Do you dare to shine even more brightly and radiantly now?

Thursday 30th

Your best bet today is to create time for meditation and to connect to the divine. Your dreams and intuition are amplified. You can feel very nurtured by making use of this energy and feel comfort that is usually hard to achieve. Keep your notebook at hand.

Friday 31st

With all the present insights, a feeling of melancholy could arise. Don't be too worried as the energy will pass. But as long as it is here, why don't you embrace it and figure out what the source of that melancholy is? It might be a critical hint regarding those core beliefs that are holding you back.

AUGUST

....

Saturday 1st

You try and understand how all these fundamental
changes need to work in your day to day reality. You
could also realise what you have changed already and
know that what's within and without constantly mirror
each other. It is a hermetic principle: as above so below,
as within so without.

Sunday 2nd

Hold on tight, the universe could throw you a curveball.
The unpredictable energy is heightened as the Moon
also moves on your sign, Aquarius. Since sometimes
even you don't know what your next action is going to
be, expect the unexpected - you are well equipped to
deal with it.

Monday 3rd

Happy Full Moon in Aquarius! Take a look in the mirror
and acknowledge yourself for all that you are, for all the
characteristics you love and those that you are at odds
with. Accept yourself the way you are. Unique, eccentric,
weird and perfect because of that. You are here on a
mission that no-one else could accomplish.

Tuesday 4th

Mars is in a discussion with Jupiter. You might find
yourself struggling to take action regarding your new
and improved beliefs. It is challenging to leave all
patterns behind and integrate new ones. It takes a while
until they run on auto-pilot. Use conscious awareness
and don't expect too much at once.

Wednesday 5th

Mercury finally leaves Cancer and enters Leo. So your
focus will be on relationships which will be appreciated
by your partner, although you most often need to have a
range of people to connect to. So it is unlikely you will
start to cling to your partner, but that doesn't mean you
are not committed.

Thursday 6th

Venus has had an extended stay in Gemini and her
mission was to transform and shine brighter than ever
before. For you, this was all about your self-expression.
She is now in conjunction with the north node, the
current focus point of evolution. Your new ways to
express yourself will guide you across the finish line.

Friday 7th

We have two energies shifting today. Venus is entering
Cancer where she focuses on beautifying and
harmonising your everyday life, and the Moon enters
Aries. The Moon and Venus get into a debate. You can
feel frustrated, eager to start with exciting things and not
want to look at the usual day to day.

Saturday 8th

At least your relationships are exciting and you will
have a fantastic day connecting and sharing. If you find
some admiration you are willing to accept it, the only
thing hard to take would be somebody stealing the show.
As long as you and your partner put each other in the
spotlight, all is fine.

Sunday 9th

You can be moody today as triggers are flying low and
lots of stuff is going on internally. It would be helpful for
the people around you if you would share some of the
things going on, instead of just drawing back. This way
they have at least a chance of understanding when you
detach unexpectedly.

Monday 10th

You can feel a little lazy and also stubborn. It will be
hard to be satisfied, and you could feel like the Princess
– or Prince – and the Pea. A little surprise might spark
your day and get you out of the dullness if you choose to
take an opportunity.

Tuesday 11th

You and your partner can be in conflict about your
home life or an issue regarding family. If you take a look
at the situation, you might notice that it reflects a battle
inside of yourself, between what you feel and what you
feel you can show.

Wednesday 12th

Your mojo is back, and you feel on track. The Moon
in Gemini allows you a more light-hearted attitude,
and you want to include your partner in your creative
plans. If their energy supports and sparks your inner
fire, go for it. Otherwise, you need to fan your inner
flame by yourself.

Thursday 13th

Intensity is the name of the game. Mars is in discussion
with Pluto, and it is hard to get your 'new' self going.
If you think about a butterfly, it had no wings as a
caterpillar and it takes a while to learn how to use them.
Impatience and force aren't good advisers.

Friday 14th

Just keep trying, perseverance is the key. Remember
that you can act very differently now. Many more
opportunities are available, and it will take a while
until you discover how powerful you actually are. Use
your visionary skills to expand your mind beyond the
common and known.

Saturday 15th

The weekend brings lots of energy and some kind of ease. You gladly learned how to nurture yourself and can recharge by sticking to your routines. This way you are able to show up in your relationship and allow your partner to see you at your best.

Sunday 16th

Your planetary guide Uranus is starting its retrograde motion, and that is a big deal. Before you can continue breaking more new ground in your home and family situation, you need to integrate and adjust what you have been working on thus far. Just one reformation at a time.

Monday 17th

The energy is hot but somehow not. You could push too hard and exhaust yourself, although you get a lot done if you are able to keep a cool head. Taking a break is essential and don't get drawn into the drama. Maybe offer some ice-cream if things get too hot at all.

Tuesday 18th

Happy New Moon in Leo! This one is perfect to set some relationship goals, declare your love which includes the love of yourself. Focus on your heart and figure out what it is that you truly desire Aquarius. Sometimes it is hard to tell your own desires from those of others.

Wednesday 19th

It is a beautiful day to go deep and focus on details. The
Sun is in a harmonious aspect to the nodes so you might
feel like you made another essential step towards your
future. You feel energetic and confident and are getting
ready for step number two by creating a plan.

Thursday 20th

A little disillusionment could strike you today. The
dream has been so beautiful, colourful, blissful. But
reality shows you a different picture that can be hard
to face. It is not always easy to take, but the blessing is
inherent. No more illusions. You can see clearly now.

Friday 21st

Time to get real and committed. Mercury enters the sign
of Virgo ahead of the Sun, and your mind is very detail
oriented and, at least for a minute, in alignment with
your emotions. You are ready to get down and focus on
all the nitty-gritty that you usually try to avoid.

Saturday 22nd

There is a time for everything and, for you, this is now a
significant period of self analysis. You can be more focused
and are under no illusions. It cannot get more real than
it currently is and you want to create results more than
anything else. Even utopia has to be rooted in reality.

Sunday 23rd

Grind down, dig deeper, give everything. Even though it is a Sunday, it is unlikely you just hang around and relax. It is more likely you have lots of energy that you channel into following your career or legacy goals. Your partner might not like it, but when you are in deep, no one can stop you.

Monday 24th

Possibly not everything turns out the way you planned it and Saturn is ready to remind you of a lesson he taught you many times. Perseverance. Get up, try again. This is a process, not a race. You cannot rush what needs effort to build. If you want a solid foundation, it just takes time. Practise patience.

Tuesday 25th

Today is a welcome change to the more severe energy of the last few days. The Moon sparks with the light of hope, and it is a lovely time to connect to your tribe. You find harmony by expanding your self-nurturing, and you might have a good idea of how to reform your home situation.

Wednesday 26th

Use the energy to meet your friends, go out or engage in meetings in your work environment. You can recharge by connecting with others, and the energy is literally asking you to do that. If nothing is going on, initiate a meeting by inviting friends to a barbecue.

Thursday 27th

What does it take, Aquarius? What does it take to move forward and release the old? You could take a vital action today and want to make sure it is following your highest intentions. Focus on a love greater than reality and tune into compassion. Take some time for yourself and reflect.

Friday 28th

Isn't it amazing how much wisdom lies within you? You can access this today and integrate another part of the current changes. You might think you have already changed enough and lots of change has already taken place. This is now some kind of finale for the remainder of 2020, and the big stuff happens at the end.

Saturday 29th

So much is going on! There's lots of grounding Earth energy that you can use to build and create something with the pieces you have already been given. It is a breakthrough day, and by tonight you can pat yourself on the shoulder. This will be a busy day, make sure you integrate some fun and laughter.

Sunday 3oth

The Moon is in your sign Aquarius and lends you some of its superpowers. Mercury is facing Neptune to check that some of what has been dreamed about appears in reality. And Venus is facing Pluto which might not be pleasant, but it is powerful nevertheless. There is beauty in transformation.

Monday 3ıst

You are able to act on your genius ideas and find just the right way to improvise in a situation. Your mind is flexible and thorough so you won't miss a detail. Move ahead fearlessly, if changes are necessary you will have enough time to implement them. If you don't try, nothing happens.

SEPTEMBER
. . . .

Tuesday 1st
This is a good day for you to focus on your resources and figure out a way to make them work. This major shift is happening because you are now able to act from a place of integrity and authenticity. This makes other people believe in your cause, so they are willing to add to your resources.

Wednesday 2nd
Happy Full Moon in Pisces. This Full Moon illuminates your resources and possessions, not only the outer ones but also the inner ones, like your physical energy. The Sun is in a harmonious connection to your planetary guide, so there is a significant shift happening in your favour.

Thursday 3rd
Mercury in alignment with Saturn results in you being able to take the right steps, acting on a plan and creating a solid foundation. It is a very useful energy that helps you out big time. The Moon in Aries fuels you with energy so you can get a lot done.

Friday 4th

You think you are now all set up regarding your health and routines, but possibly there is an issue you didn't see coming. Frustration could be high but try to use this new awareness to create a solution. Just set up another plan and stick to it and you will be fine.

Saturday 5th

This was a quick run-through Aquarius, Mercury is already moving forward and is now focusing on your vision, philosophy and higher education. What do you need to learn to move ahead, and what is your current philosophy. It might be a good idea to sit with that and write it down.

Sunday 6th

It seems like Venus thinks it is hip to be square. She is again shifting signs and is again square to the Moon just as she enters. This time the energy is more about sustaining what you have already got, and how to use that as you walk towards your vision.

Monday 7th

Overall, this day has a stabilising effect with just a minor shake-up. You have been wondering how you can be more authentic in your family, and it seems like you finally figured out how you can expand with them instead of without.

Tuesday 8th

At the beginning of the day, you might be moody and feel challenged by family demands. You need to remain calm and focused. Later today, the Moon shifts into Gemini and this is an energy you can thrive on. It brings joy and fun in your world and you really need that right now.

Wednesday 9th

Sun-Jupiter days are the best as you may know by now. If you want to start something new or get a project to the next level, you couldn't get better energy to do it than Sun and Jupiter in Earth signs with the ability and stamina to ground and bring everything to fruition. Don't waste this energy.

Thursday 10th

Mars is going retrograde in your area of learning, siblings and immediate surroundings. As Mars is in his home sign, you might feel the energy intensively. It is not a time to move ahead, it is more time to readjust. For you, it could also be about moving to another place.

Friday 11th

The Sun is shining a light on Neptune and asks you to focus on reality while chasing your dreams. Reality checks are necessary, so you know where you can start from. You can have a tendency to believe that everything will fly towards you automatically. Instead, you have an easy time if you just put the effort in.

Saturday 12th

Inner needs and outer needs: what is more important?
The truth is they are equally important. Today asks you
to find equilibrium by listening to your inner voice and
acting on the outside. If you take the right action, you
can feel very comfortable and nurtured by tonight.

Sunday 13th

Jupiter changes direction and will move forward again!
This is big because that means the Jupiter-Capricorn
story is about to end and Jupiter is more than happy
about that. No more dealing with restrictions, instead
it's time for expansion. But first some more stretching
of the current structures.

Monday 14th

The Moon meets Venus, so there is some harmony and
lots of love in your relationships. The Sun and Pluto are
in a harmonious connection, and you can reorganise
powerfully and effectively. With this new setup, you are
able to follow your plans more actively than before.

Tuesday 15th

Venus square to Uranus might indicate a conflict with
your partner about your home situation. Moon in Virgo
deepens your focus but also your perfectionism, and you
need to be careful about getting too picky. Once again
you are asked to make a choice between clinging to the
past or moving towards the future?

Wednesday 16th

You are still getting a lot of the nitty-gritty done and could really need a little love or laughter. You could get too deep into all the details and lose the bigger picture. Spend some time with your partner or a friend to counterbalance all the mental energy.

Thursday 17th

Happy New Moon in Virgo. This one is wonderful for deciding what resources you want to receive and use during the next six months. You have a very analytical approach, and this might take you a long way. Being too sceptical could lead to missed opportunities.

Friday 18th

Dedication and perseverance are vital. The Sun and Saturn are in a harmonious connection, and this means you can put down some more building blocks. With the Moon in discussion with Jupiter you want to make your vision even more prominent and broad. This is important as it keeps you motivated.

Saturday 19th

Where is your journey taking you? Is your current environment the one in which you can follow your vision and bring it to life? There is something about the bigger picture that is still in conflict with your beliefs. Some of them are still holding you back; improvement is necessary.

Sunday 20th

You want to focus on work on a Sunday, but family demands can distract you. You could become annoyed and feel challenged to meet all needs. The chances are you will give in and act on the family demands first. This will make you angry, but you will only realise it once you have made a choice.

Monday 21st

You start the week full of happiness and optimism and with the desire to connect to your social groups and tribes. This most often inspires and recharges you. The other part of this day is that you might need to make some adjustment to your vision, which can feel difficult.

Tuesday 22nd

Welcome to the Autumn Equinox. Day and night are equal so there is a maximum balance. For you, the energetic focus is on your vision quest, foreign travel and the foreign in general. How can you balance your need for stability and being rooted with your desire to experience the new and unusual?

Wednesday 23rd

There is something that you are blindsided by. Somehow you don't get the message. Your insecurities can keep you from moving ahead and trusting that the outcome will be favourable. Don't allow the scale to tip in the wrong direction. Instead ask yourself: what is the lesson of your doubts?

Thursday 24th

Sometimes you want to stay where you are, and
sometimes you want to go far out of your comfort zone,
far out into the unknown. With Mercury in discussion
with Mars retrograde, you try to adjust these different
needs. What if you decided to root elsewhere?

Friday 25th

There are hardly any breaks, and it is a great idea to be
gentle with yourself today. If you can get home early and
have some time out, you should. Going for a walk can
help you to sort your mind and come to a place of
inner stillness.

Saturday 26th

The Moon is entering your sign in the morning hours, so
it is quite an energetic shift from yesterday's seriousness.
The Moon makes a harmonious connection to the Sun,
so you have lots of good energy for connecting and
relating. It is possible you are taking part in a good cause.

Sunday 27th

You could find yourself up late because your mind
is restless and you have had a big revelation. Surely
this could also happen in your dreams. Better keep
your notebook handy. Mercury is changing gears and
enters Scorpio. Here he becomes a detective ready to
investigate and dig deep.

Monday 28th

You can start the week still thriving in your energy
and ready to have all the critical meetings and talks.
You show your best attitude and are also willing to go
beyond the superficial and ask more in-depth questions
than usual. Later today the energy shifts and your
imagination is high.

Tuesday 29th

Drum roll, please! Saturn stations direct. This is a
significant turning point Aquarius. No more replanning
and restructuring. You will put the finishing touches to
your foundation, and this one will continue to carry you
through the next thirty years. The other goods news is
that you also come to an agreement with your partner
regarding your home situation.

Wednesday 30th

Some final challenges need to be faced. Can your stand
the test? Are you really committed, is there reliability
and integrity? If yes, good for you, you are on the right
track. If not, what keeps you from having integrity? You
have all the resources needed.

OCTOBER

. . . .

Thursday 1st
Happy Full Moon in Aries. This Full Moon highlights what you have learned with regard to new communications, and it is also a great moment to have a look at your environment and make a stock-check. What is worth holding onto and what should you release to move ahead enthusiastically?

Friday 2nd
The Venus in Virgo transit will be an interesting one this year as it will allow you some of the seeds you set out to grow. You focus on being useful and can have access to further resources. Venus is about money so some cash might come your way.

Saturday 3rd
Venus connects to the Moon in Taurus, and that is supportive energy coming from your home and family. It could also be you stocking up the resources to sustain your family and maybe a new home. However, this is definitely some good news and a win on both sides.

Sunday 4th

Why do you like to get into work on Sundays, Aquarius? Maybe because it is your way of bringing in the unexpected, although everyone who knows you can expect that already. Anyway, this can still bring up conflict with your family so how do you want to handle it this time?

Monday 5th

Pluto, the planet of transformation, destruction and resurrection, is moving direct again. You can be assured that for now you have broken enough structures and can focus on using the scattered pieces in a new way. Other than that, today's vibe is about seeking comfort and pleasure, and possibly good food.

Tuesday 6th

The Moon is in Gemini, while the Sun is in Libra. Yes, please. Get out a pen and paper, brushes, pencils and start to create. You don't need to focus on a specific outcome, just do it for the sheer joy, and you will be delighted with what you can create if there is no pressure at all.

Wednesday 7th

Your family may have a surprise in store, or something is revealed at work that has an unexpected effect on your home life. This could be about a relocation, business travel or a promotion. Don't rush the decision and if you can, ponder it over the next month and during the upcoming Mercury retrograde.

Thursday 8th

The Moon is moving into Cancer and making tense
aspects to the Sun and to everything in Capricorn. So
there are many mood swings, and you feel somehow
busy all the time. Balance is today's goal so stick to your
routines and activities that add to your self-nurturing.

Friday 9th

It is the second of three discussions Mars and Pluto are
having. This time Mars is retrograde and Pluto is moving
ahead, so you try to adjust your actions to the ongoing
transformation. You are acting more carefully and
possibly very differently from your first attempt, so act
upon your deepest desires.

Saturday 10th

Venus is in an easy conversation with Uranus, and you
might receive some money or are able to access some
resources provided by your family. It is an unexpected
blessing, and you are not yet sure how to handle it as
everything has happened quickly. Breathe and count to ten.

Sunday 11th

Are you ready to expand your vision just a little more?
Or even a whole lot more? The Sun and Jupiter are in a
challenging aspect and they ask you to surpass yourself.
This aspect is a blessing in disguise because most often
we need to overcome an obstacle to realise how much
more we are capable of.

Monday 12th

The Moon is in Leo, and you connect to the nodes while
you enjoy spending time with your partner and at least
for today don't consider anything else more important.
It is rare to have your undivided attention, so why not
make it more special with a generous gift?

Tuesday 13th

The Sun is in a tug-of-war with Mars retrograde. Many
options seem to be available, but what is the right one
to act upon? Sticking with the old environment or
trying your luck somewhere new? With the Moon in
Virgo, you look at all the needs your family has and try
to create a plan.

Wednesday 14th

The entire topic of your work and legacy needs further
investigation. There might still be things hidden from
you, and you need to rethink, investigate and ponder it a
lot. Mercury retrograde is here to help you out and give
you the perfect setup to do that. Three weeks to gain
clarity lie ahead.

Thursday 15th

The Sun is in another discussion with Pluto. Are you
already making use of your power and adjusting your
vision? Or are you still playing too small? Dare to go for
the big view and the big picture Aquarius. The effort is
needed anyway so why go for something small if you
could also achieve the real deal?

Friday 16th

Happy New Moon in Libra. This is the perfect time to review your visions and see where you are. Perhaps you could make a mind-map to work out what truly inspires you. Put it somewhere in your sight, in a place where you can see it daily.

Saturday 17th

This Saturday, your mind and heart align, and you come to a place of inner peace and stillness. There is still a lot to figure out, but at least you don't feel torn apart any longer. Something previously hidden might come to the surface, and it is likely a critical moment for your upcoming decision.

Sunday 18th

The Sun has lots of discussions these days, and this one is with Saturn. It is about sticking with the rules and making sure that all dreams have a chance to be realised. You will need patience because you cannot rush the process, but if you show up and take one step at a time, the rewards will be granted.

Monday 19th

There is exciting energy, as Jupiter is in a fluid connection to Venus and in a stressful one with Mars. So you are making plans on how to expand in an organised fashion but are not yet ready to act upon those plans which are frustrating. A good counterbalance is to meet with your friends and have some fun.

Tuesday 20th

Mercury retrograde is now facing your planetary guide
Uranus, as if to ask for another big revelation or insight.
It might be a perfect time to discuss the upcoming
and possible changes with your family to consider
their point of view. It helps you to see everything from
another perspective.

Wednesday 21st

The overall tone is severe today, and you are mainly busy
with yourself. A good vibration is coming from Venus in a
harmonious connection to Pluto. This is about being able
to use your power appropriately for a more significant
cause and to make use of the resources at hand.

Thursday 22nd

The Sun is entering your area of vocation, legacy and
career. A major decision will come up during that transit.
Patience is a virtue, and you might need to breathe deep
often because you desperately want to move ahead but
it's not the time. Use the chance to rework and refigure
the things you have already worked on.

Friday 23rd

It is perfect energy for a Friday. You are able to focus on
work in the morning and once your leisure time arrives
the energy opens up and you have time to experiment
and feel as independent as your heart desires. The Moon
is in your sign Aquarius so just enjoy the energy in
alignment with yourself.

Saturday 24th

Another solution is knocking at your door. You might have found new resources that you can invest in building your new structures. With Saturn and Venus both in Earth energy and in signs that deal with responsibility, discernment and practicability, you have green lights for moving ahead with this part of the plan.

Sunday 25th

Mercury is back in the heart of the Sun, waiting to receive insights about your career situation. With the Moon in Pisces and the easy connection to Scorpio, it is possible that your dreams have some messages and ideas rising from the depth of your subconscious into your consciousness.

Monday 26th

Dream life is enhanced and so is your desire to have a bit of magic in your life. It would be a great time to watch a movie, read a book or go to the theatre. Nothing major is happening, which is a welcome shift and allows you to take a breath.

Tuesday 27th

More magic and more rest, please. The energy is continuously chill, and you can lie around and dream about utopia without feeling guilty. Make sure you still follow your routines to stay grounded and know that tomorrow's energy will be very different. So enjoy the time to retreat.

Wednesday 28th

Mercury retrogrades back into Libra, so it seems like you need to take a look at your long term aims and make some adjustments. Venus is also moving into Libra, where she loves to be, so you can be sure lots of harmony is coming your way. It is time to focus on the people that accompany you.

Thursday 29th

Connect to your neighbours or your sibling today as there might be an important message or hint hidden in the conversations you conduct. This hint will help you out with further adjustments, and with regards to the decisions you have to make about your career and the environment you want to live in.

Friday 30th

Lots of Earth energy is around and after dealing with lots of issues in the morning, the energy eases, and you can have a beautiful and chilled-out evening within the family circle. Going out for a family dinner would be an excellent way to add some extravagance to your day.

Saturday 31st

If you've been seeking to try something new, or to make changes in your life, then today might be the perfect time to begin. The Full Moon is likely to present new opportunities from turning over a new leaf to unexpected invitations. Be sure to look within for answers if you're unsure which step to take.

NOVEMBER

. . . .

Sunday 1st

There is an unexpected development happening in
your career and home situation. But you are full of an
undeniable optimism that the solution will present itself.
Good! Don't allow others to alter your perspective.
They might not be open-minded enough to see the
situation resolve.

Monday 2nd

The safety you experience in your family is built on a
solid foundation and will last and carry you through
no matter where you go. You just need to be aware that
being rooted is not the same as being stuck. When the
Moon shifts into Gemini this evening it is time to have
some joy and laughter.

Tuesday 3rd

It is important to know who is on your team. Who are
the people who thrive on your ideas and vice versa?
Who are the ones that can dream the same dream as
you can? Make sure you spend the most time relating to
supporters and be supportive in return.

Wednesday 4th

Congratulations on having had such a hard look at your career choices and opportunities. You did enough rethinking and refiguring, and Mercury is now moving direct. With the Moon on the North Node, you feel ready to make a proper choice and set sails to the future.

Thursday 5th

It is possible that you feel afraid to follow your vision. What if you would be all on your own? What if you cannot stick to your routines or fail to nurture yourself? There is no need to be afraid. You have the flexibility to create routines in a different environment.

Friday 6th

What would you actually have to change and adjust in order to function in a new environment? What is necessary for you to feel safe and nurtured? Consider internal and external security. What is required to make you feel comfortable? For each and everyone there are individual factors that create a feeling of being at home. Which ones are yours?

Saturday 7th

This weekend you might pack up with your partner and go on a trip. Seeing something different and making sure you are seen too. It won't be the super romantic just snuggling in the sheets style of weekend, but more about visiting museums or even attending a banquet.

Sunday 8th

Where and how you show up at today's event can be important for your public image. You could run into somebody by coincidence, or it would also be possible that you merely forgot to tell your partner that this is a business meeting? This might cause some tension. Let your charm play and your heart show.

Monday 9th

Monday morning and you are still high as a kite from the weekend energy, which was a real boost to your self-esteem. It might be a little hard to focus in the morning, but in the afternoon you are back on track and can start to take care of some important details.

Tuesday 10th

Today, Mercury is back on the edge of Libra, so you can have some final thoughts about your vision and then it is all about integrating them in your career and legacy. It is a significant chance, and you are the only person who knows if you dare to take it. But do you want to ask the "what if?" question?

Wednesday 11th

You have an analytical look at the current situation and are able to commit, as you see everything is in perfect alignment and you are almost ready to get up and go. It has been a long time coming, but you feel like something is shifting soon and you are right.

Thursday 12th

The best things come in threes. This is the final meeting of Jupiter and Pluto, this time under Saturn's beady eye. Now they get it right, and you are finally able to unite your deepest desires with your highest intentions and… the sky is the limit.

Friday 13th

It is a day of final and minimal adjustments before once again the energy shifts to your legacy and career, Aquarius. It is possible that you spend this weekend contemplating, but one never knows what you will come up with. Once you are in your creative genius mode, you dive in deep and gone you are.

Saturday 14th

Finally, the day has come. You have been so frustrated during these last months where you felt stuck and like you could not move ahead, but instead needed to redo lots of things. Now Mars is moving direct again. A big relief and time to make the change happen.

Sunday 15th

Happy New Moon in Scorpio. It is perfect and seems to be the divinely guided new beginning to set you up for your career, vocation and legacy. Set your goals regarding your public image, the impact you want to have in the world and how you want to be perceived.

Monday 16th

It is time for a little break, Aquarius. You are not
always so committed and willing to do the work
without taking a break, but that is with good reason
as too much of what is seen as "hard work" just leaves
you dry like a flower without water. Refresh by adding
vision and creativity.

Tuesday 17th

Watch out! Mercury is back in opposition to your
planetary guide and what comes up today will reveal the
choice you have already made. With the Moon on the
south node, you are able to see which social circles you
need to disconnect from. This choice doesn't come easy
but is well considered.

Wednesday 18th

It is time for action: unbelievable, but true! Remember to
act from a place of integrity and inner authority. You need
to be willing to take full responsibility, put in every effort
and be disciplined and show up every single day. The next
month might feel like snail speed, but you are moving.

Thursday 19th

Today's energy is serious, constructive and vital. It is
like a final and official approval. This can come from
the outside, like a boss or another authority figure, or it
could be from your inner authority. Don't underestimate
the effect your self-validation has. It is huge.

Friday 20th

Shake it up and shake yourself a little loose, Aquarius. Be a rebel today and allow yourself to do everything differently, just to have some alternation. Have your afternoon tea for breakfast, brush your teeth with your left hand, use the train if you usually go by car. You will for sure have a thousand ideas.

Saturday 21st

Today's energy is beautiful once again sees two significant shifts. The Sun is entering Sagittarius, willing to bring in your new tribe, and is supported by Venus enhancing your work-related relationships. The Moon on the north node brings some necessary energy. Exciting!

Sunday 22nd

Use this Sunday to hang loose, recharge and drift away in daydreams. Wear your unicorn onesie or something that adds a sense of magic to your day and escape into fantasy land, via book, movie or audio. It could be a beautiful autumn day, so getting out in nature might be a good idea, too.

Monday 23rd

Empathy and compassion are high. It is not a day for making tough choices but to listen carefully to what your fellow human beings have to say. You can read between the lines today and hear what is not even mentioned. It might be difficult to differentiate which emotions are your own.

Tuesday 24th

You are still very tuned in to a higher consciousness. There might be lots of signs and synchronicities, you just need to see them and figure out what they mean. The universe is telling you that you are on the right path. Dreams can hold messages again, so try to remember them as well as you can.

Wednesday 25th

Wouldn't it be nice to organise a little feast with your friends or in your neighbourhood? You are willing to take the initiative and get out the invitations. It will be a lovely meeting, and you will have lots of inspiring conversations.

Thursday 26th

You are unstoppable today, ready to take various actions and focus on your goals and your development. You are able to control your mood swings and keep pushing forward, which might help your co-workers to do the same. Be bold and courageous!

Friday 27th

Venus in opposition to your planetary guide Uranus can make or break the deal. The deal is created when you feel safe and comfortable, the deal will break if there is even the tiniest amount of distrust. If you are in you are in. Listen to your inner voice. It is whispering the answer all the time.

Saturday 28th

Nothing too major happening, you could say it is a usual
Saturday, which actually makes it an unusual one for
you, because how many ordinary Saturdays are there for
you? Anyway, the most exciting thing could be reading a
new book or watching a new movie. Relax!

Sunday 29th

Another laid-back day, at least speaking about outside
appearances. There might be a family dinner or lunch
which you enjoy, but inside there is something brewing.
Mercury and Jupiter are in a harmonious connection
which lights up your mood and expands your mind.
Only the deep and complex themes are exciting today.

Monday 3oth

The month ends with a partial Lunar Eclipse in Gemini.
It is a potent, somehow fated and yet stable energy
supported by a connection from Mercury to Saturn. Take
a look at the last six months, you have taken many steps
toward your future. It might have looked like nothing
happened, but it was a lot. Kudos to you!

DECEMBER

....

Tuesday 1st

It is the beginning of the final month this year and wouldn't you think the energy would calm down? Major energy shifts are coming up, and you won't have a dull moment. The Moon is with the north node pointing towards the future while Mercury enters Sagittarius and you focus on the bigger picture and your tribe.

Wednesday 2nd

You are a little sensitive today and need to listen to your feelings. Maybe with all that excitement and everything you tried to figure out, you did not take the time just to feel. Let all the emotions rise up today and do everything to make yourself feel comfortable.

Thursday 3rd

Consider what you learned about nurturing yourself this year. Some actions and routines proved themselves more important than others. What do you want to learn and could you make a start now? You know all the answers inside, what works for you might not be what works for others.

Friday 4th

The Moon enters Leo later today and combines with the Sun and Mercury in Sagittarius. It is amazing energy for gatherings with friends and your partner. You can have a lovely time, amazing conversations and tell tale after tale. You might end up being the entertainer at the party.

Saturday 5th

A little family conflict could disturb the otherwise peaceful Saturday mood. If you don't make mountains out of molehills, this can be resolved quickly. Other than that you will want to be out and about and spread some gifts in your neighbourhood. Neighbourly help clearly counts and is highly appreciated.

Sunday 6th

Focus on the love, Aquarius. Any kind of love. Self-love, earthly love and divine and unconditional love. You do want to spread some love today, and you can do best if you come from a place of trust. Focus on feeling, without trying to analyse how each love vibration is defined.

Monday 7th

Something more tangible is on the table today. You do a check up on your finances and might figure out that there is more available than you thought because your family unexpectedly added to them. This is excellent news. You might take a second look to be sure, but then you allow gratitude to take over.

127

Tuesday 8th

It feels terrific to be set up, and you could burst with joy because of that. You are highly optimistic and might spread good vibrations for many people in your life. Memorise that feeling Aquarius, this is what it feels like when you are in alignment within yourself.

Wednesday 9th

Be very cautious during the next few days. You could fall for illusions. If something seems to be too good to be true, it most likely is. All is not gold that glitters. There are some very well done fakes, and there are also people wearing masks.

Thursday 10th

Watch out, there could still be some deception going on. If you follow your instincts and use your investigative attitude, you can easily expose the person under suspicion. It will be harder to tell if you are the one deceiving yourself and falling for an illusion. Take a hard look at reality.

Friday 11th

It is time to say goodbye to some social circles and groups. They might have helped you out a lot, entertained you and broadened your mind, but on your new road, you need some new people. Say goodbye properly, have an honourable, respectful ending and don't run away.

Saturday 12th

The Moon is meeting Venus, and you could have a final meet and greet with some of the people you are leaving behind. It is most likely related to your work or legacy so it could be some co-workers or people from a club or a charity. Show your gratitude.

Sunday 13th

The Moon in Sagittarius is also asking for engagement: you will be out and about and in meetings again. Spare yourself some time and think about your development and what you could teach others from your experience. You have achieved some kind of wisdom, and you should not keep it for yourself.

Monday 14th

Happy New Moon in Sagittarius. This New Moon has a super optimistic vibe with Jupiter and Venus connected to it. You can set the intentions for your new adventure, and this is just some days away! Declare that you will look on the bright side of life and commit to the people supporting and joining you.

Tuesday 15th

Your optimism sparks your actions and Venus is now joining the other planets in Sagittarius. There is such a big emphasis of hope and faith and joyful energy, it is Christmas spirit at its best. You do need to take a little time for yourself, and you had better do it today and tomorrow because oh so much is coming down the pipeline!

Wednesday 16th

It is unlikely that you will find a state of calmness and peace today because the energy is so exciting and feels more like you fidget around on your chair. Find some time for meditation, a walk outside can be meditative as well. Connect to your core and know you have access to your inner power.

Thursday 17th

The trumpets call, Saturn is leaving Capricorn for good! He is now entering your own sign, Aquarius and this is a massive turning point. This transit will keep you busy during the next two and a half years, and it is the beginning of a new era. You can now begin to anchor in the new and be the reformer and revolutionary you came to be.

Friday 18th

Mercury is *Cazimi*, in the heart of the Sun for the final time in 2020. That this happens in Sagittarius will only unleash more hope and optimism. It is a beautiful set up for a new cycle. The Moon connects to the north node, so it is a little like New Year has come early.

Saturday 19th

Are you ready for the next massive shift? Yes, there is more to come. Jupiter is on the final degree of Capricorn and can't wait to get out of there and slip into Aquarius. This has been an uncomfortable space for him, dealing with lots of restriction, but at least he could share his wisdom and you learned a lot.

Sunday 20th

One more biggie before Christmas. Jupiter now in Aquarius is ready to give you a boost on self-confidence and growth you haven't seen for a while. Saturn is here awaiting him, and as they both join forces, they set you up for significant achievements, improvements, inventions and the revolution.

Monday 21st

The Sun enters Capricorn. For you, this brings a focus on self-reflection, but this year it will be so much easier for you, as there is only Pluto sitting in that area and all the other weight has gone. You can sigh in relief and get ready for a relatively calm Capricorn season.

Tuesday 22nd

All these shifts and changes have been quite a lot to deal with, and you don't know if you are coming or going. Take a breath and think about Christmas. Is there anything you need to prepare, shop or get ready? Focus on something small for now, do your best and don't stress out.

Wednesday 23rd

The third and final time that Mars and Pluto square each other. It is about acting on your deepest desires and moving in the right direction. As both planets move forward this time, you are finally progressing, too. Find the time to meditate and listen to your inner voice to guide you.

Thursday 24th

Christmas Eve is here, and you will most likely want to spend this with your family and chosen family. As the Moon is in Taurus, everything is set up to be comfortable and classy. It is likely to be calm, the only thing to remember is you can also agree to disagree if opinions differ.

Friday 25th

Merry Christmas, Aquarius! The Moon is crossing
your planetary guide, and Uranus is always good for
a surprise. Maybe a family member has some happy
surprise news. Christmas gifts count as a surprise too
so it will be a peaceful day with jolly conversations and
hopefully amazing food to indulge in.

Saturday 26th

Boxing day, and you need a little space to retreat. Take
some time for yourself if possible. When you are around
others, put the focus on the spirit of Christmas and feel
not only the love but also the magic. It is a day to be
peaceful and relax.

Sunday 27th

Even though it is Sunday, you have had enough rest and
want some fun and action. You could want to go out,
dance or start to dive into creative endeavours. At least,
if you find the time, as your phone could constantly be
ringing and you will agree on spontaneous visits.

Monday 28th

The Sun is in a harmonious connection to your
planetary guide, while the Moon is with the north node.
An unexpected door is opening for you and all you need
to do is walk through. This is in alignment with your
future path so grab your luck by the scruff of its neck.

Tuesday 29th

Happy Full Moon in Cancer. Interesting that the year
started and ends with a Cancer Full Moon. See how
much you evolved during this year regarding self-
nurturing and confronting your feelings. It is a great
deal to feel emotionally safe within yourself. This allows
you to relate in freedom.

Wednesday 30th

There needs to be compassion and surrender. You
cannot always push ahead, sometimes you need to trust
the process and that there are higher forces involved.
You have learned a lot but never forget that even though
you are open-minded, you cannot see the entire picture.
There will always be something hidden.

Thursday 31st

Welcome to New Year's Eve, Aquarius. What a year it
has been! Massive, profound, challenging, intense,
exciting and you did surpass yourself. When you move
forward to your future, never forget the lessons learned.
Great things are awaiting you, and you can make a
huge difference in the upcoming years.

Aquarius

. . . .

PEOPLE WHO
SHARE YOUR SIGN

PEOPLE WHO
SHARE YOUR SIGN
....

Born to be different and shake things up, Aquarians
are the liberating Air sign that are prepared to ruffle
some feathers if needed. From the speeches of Abraham
Lincoln to the words of Virginia Woolf, the unique
insight and intellect that so many Aquarians have
make them a sign to be listened to and take notice of.
Discover which of these individualist Aquarians share
your exact birthday with and see if you can spot
the similarities.

January 21st
BooBoo Stewart (1994), Jerry Trainor (1977), Emma
Bunton (1976), Geena Davis (1956), Paul Allen (1953), Billy
Ocean (1950), Plácido Domingo (1941), Benny Hill (1924),
Christian Dior (1905), Grigori Rasputin (1869-1916)

January 22nd
Silentó (1998), Logic (1990), Hidetoshi Nakata (1977),
Gabriel Macht (1972), Guy Fieri (1968), Diane Lane (1965),
Linda Blair (1959), Steve Perry (1949), John Hurt (1940)

January 23rd
Doutzen Kroes (1985), Draya Michele (1985), Arjen
Robben (1984), Tito Ortiz (1975), Tiffani Thiessen (1974),
Mariska Hargitay (1964), Princess Caroline of Monaco
(1957), Richard Dean Anderson (1950), Édouard Manet
(1832)

January 24th
Luis Suárez (1987), Mischa Barton (1986), Justin Baldoni
(1984), Frankie Grande (1983), Tatyana Ali (1979), Kristen
Schaal (1978), Ed Helms (1974), Kenya Moore (1971),
Sharon Tate (1943)

January 25th
Calum Hood (1996), Robinho (1984), Alicia Keys (1981),
Xavi (1980), Charlene, Princess of Monaco (1978), Virginia
Woolf (1882)

January 26th
Colin O'Donoghue (1981), Brendan Rodgers (1973), José
Mourinho (1963), Wayne Gretzky (1961), Ellen DeGeneres
(1958), Eddie Van Halen (1955), Angela Davis (1944), Paul
Newman (1925), Louis Zamperini (1917), Maria von Trapp
(1905)

January 27th
Rosamund Pike (1979), Patton Oswalt (1969), Alan
Cumming (1965), Bridget Fonda (1964), Narciso
Rodriguez (1961), Mimi Rogers (1956), Mikhail
Baryshnikov (1948), Beatrice Tinsley (1941), Lewis Carroll
(1832)

January 28th
Ariel Winter (1998), Will Poulter (1993), J. Cole (1985),
Elijah Wood (1981), Nick Carter (1980), Gianluigi Buffon
(1978), Rick Ross (1976), Carlos Slim (1940), Alan Alda (1936)

January 29th

Adam Lambert (1982), Sara Gilbert (1975), Heather
Graham (1970), Oprah Winfrey (1954), Tom Selleck (1945),
Katharine Ross (1940), Anton Chekhov (1860)

January 30th

Eiza González (1990), Arda Turan (1987), Wilmer
Valderrama (1980), Christian Bale (1974), Phil Collins
(1951), Dick Cheney, 46th U.S. Vice President (1941),
Franklin D. Roosevelt, 32nd U.S. President (1882),

January 31st

Amy Jackson (1992), Marcus Mumford (1987), Justin
Timberlake (1981), Kerry Washington (1977), Portia
de Rossi (1973), Minnie Driver (1970), Daniel Moder
(1969), John Lydon (1956), Jonathan Banks (1947), Carol
Channing (1921), Jackie Robinson (1919), Baba Vanga (1911)

February 1st

Harry Styles (1994), Heather Morris (1987), Ronda Rousey (1987), Lauren Conrad (1986), Abbi Jacobson (1984), Michael C. Hall (1971), Lisa Marie Presley (1968), Princess Stephanie of Monaco (1965), Langston Hughes (1902), Clark Gable (1901)

February 2nd

Gerard Piqué (1987), Gemma Arterton (1986), Gemma Collins (1981), Christine Bleakley (1979), Shakira (1977), Christie Brinkley (1954), Duncan Bannatyne (1949), Farrah Fawcett (1947), David Jason (1940), Ayn Rand (1905), James Joyce (1882)

February 3rd

Sean Kingston (1990), Elizabeth Holmes (1984), Amal Clooney (1978), Isla Fisher (1976), Warwick Davis (1970), Maura Tierney (1965), Joachim Löw (1960), Nathan Lane (1956), Blythe Danner (1943), Norman Rockwell (1894)

February 4th

Hannibal Buress (1983), Gavin DeGraw (1977), Cam'ron (1976), Natalie Imbruglia (1975), Oscar De La Hoya (1973), Alice Cooper (1948), Rosa Parks (1913), Charles Lindbergh (1902)

February 5th
Neymar (1992), Darren Criss (1987), Kevin Gates (1986),
Cristiano Ronaldo (1985), Carlos Tevez (1984), Tiwa
Savage (1980), Bobby Brown (1969), Michael Sheen
(1969), Laura Linney (1964), Duff McKagan (1964),
Jennifer Jason Leigh (1962)

February 6th
Tinashe (1993), Dane DeHaan (1986), Alice Eve (1982),
Rick Astley (1966), Axl Rose (1962), Kathy Najimy (1957),
Bob Marley (1945), Ronald Reagan, 40th US President
(1911), Babe Ruth (1895)

February 7th
Bea Miller (1999), Jacksepticeye (1990), Deborah Ann
Woll (1985), Ashton Kutcher (1978), Chris Rock (1965),
Garth Brooks (1962), Eddie Izzard (1962), James Spader
(1960), Laura Ingalls Wilder (1876), Charles Dickens (1812)

February 8th
Klay Thompson (1990), Seth Green (1974), Mauricio
Macri, President of Argentina (1959), Mary Steenburgen
(1953), John Williams (1932), James Dean (1931), Dmitri
Mendeleev (1834), Jules Verne (1828)

February 9th

Michael B. Jordan (1987), Rose Leslie (1987), Tom
Hiddleston (1981), Zhang Ziyi (1979), Charlie Day (1976),
Amber Valletta (1974), Chris Gardner (1954), Mia Farrow
(1945), Alice Walker (1944), Joe Pesci (1943), Carole King
(1942)

February 10th

Chloë Grace Moretz (1997), Emma Roberts (1991),
Radamel Falcao (1986), Uzo Aduba (1981), Stephanie
Beatriz (1981), Holly Willoughby (1981), Don Omar (1978),
Elizabeth Banks (1974), Laura Dern (1967), Bertolt Brecht
(1898)

February 11th

Taylor Lautner (1992), Natalie Dormer (1982), Kelly
Rowland (1981), Damian Lewis (1971), Jennifer Aniston
(1969), Sarah Palin (1964), Crow (1962), Burt Reynolds
(1936), Leslie Nielsen (1926), Thomas Edison (1847)

February 12th

Mike Posner (1988), Iko Uwais (1983), Gucci Mane (1980),
Christina Ricci (1980), Naseem Hamed (1974), Josh Brolin
(1968), Chris McCandless (1968), Charles Darwin (1809),
Abraham Lincoln, 16th U.S. President (1809)

February 13th
Memphis Depay (1994), Mena Suvari (1979), Katie Hopkins (1975), Robbie Williams (1974), Kelly Hu (1968), Peter Gabriel (1950), Jerry Springer (1944), Kim Novak (1933)

February 14th
Freddie Highmore (1992), Ángel Di María (1988), Edinson Cavani (1987), Danai Gurira (1978), Jim Jefferies (1977), Rob Thomas (1972), Simon Pegg (1970), Michael Bloomberg (1942)

February 15th
Gary Clark Jr. (1984), Alex Borstein (1971), Shepard Fairey (1970), Chris Farley (1964), Matt Groening (1954), Janice Dickinson (1955), Jane Seymour (1951), Irena Sendler (1874), Susan B. Anthony (1820)

February 16th
The Weeknd (1990), Elizabeth Olsen (1989), Valentino Rossi (1979), Philipp Plein (1978), Amanda Holden (1971), Christopher Eccleston (1964), John McEnroe (1959), Ice-T (1958), Eckhart Tolle (1948)

February 17th

Marc Márquez (1993), Ed Sheeran (1991), Bonnie Wright (1991), Joseph Gordon-Levitt (1981), Paris Hilton (1981), Billie Joe Armstrong (1972), Denise Richards (1971), Michael Jordan (1963), Rene Russo (1954)

February 18th

Le'Veon Bell (1992), Jeremy Allen White (1991), Jillian Michaels (1974), Molly Ringwald (1968), Dr. Dre (1965), Matt Dillon (1964), John Travolta (1954), Cybill Shepherd (1950), Paco Rabanne (1934), Yoko Ono (1933), Toni Morrison (1931), Enzo Ferrari (1898)

February 19th

Mauro Icardi (1993), Victoria Justice (1993), Arielle Kebbel (1985), David Gandy (1980), Seal (1963), Benicio del Toro (1957), Jeff Daniels (1955), Tony Iommi (1948), Cristina Fernández de Kirchner, Former President of Argentina (1953)